How to imagine

(more effectively)

Practical advice on finding good ideas

Alan Taylor

First published in 2023 by Alan Taylor, London UK, and on
Kindle Direct Publishing, Seattle WA.

alan.taylor@dpmail.co.uk
www.alan-taylor.website
Text: copyright © Alan Taylor 2023
Image and cover design: copyright © Emily Taylor 2023

Cover image and design:
Emily Taylor

British Library Cataloguing-in-Publication Data
A catalogue record for this book is available from the British
Library

Library of Congress Control Number: 2023905580

ISBN 978-1-7393615-0-1 (hbk)
ISBN 978-1-7393615-1-8 (pbk)
ISBN 978-1-7393615-2-5 (ebk)

Acknowledgements:

Many thanks to the following friends and family members for practical help, advice, encouragement, and listening to me talking about the book: Kate Quarry, Emily Taylor, Litha Efthymiou, Rob Foreman, and Neil Jackson, and also to the supervisors of the PhD research on which this book draws, Professors Paul Barker and Maria Delgado of the Central School of Speech and Drama.

About the author

Alan Taylor has worked as a geography academic, an advisor on election-night coverage for British TV programmes, and as a UK civil servant, local government officer, and recycling consultant. Since ceasing paid work years ago he has become an organizer and performer in community music, founding musical ensembles and setting up the Herne Hill Music Festival. He returned to academic study in 2006, gaining an MMus and PhD in composition, and has had several papers published in academic journals. This book began life as part of his PhD studies, as did his previous book, *The Imagination of Experiences,* published by Routledge in 2021.

Table of Contents

Imagining is a skill

'You', the reader of this book, probably have to come up with ideas in your work or activities. You may need to write text of one kind or another, to produce visual images, or to imagine as a manager how to run or develop your business or activity. You might be working out the week's menus, thinking how to give a talk or perform a piece of music, replanning your garden, or designing a building. The arguments and advice in this book are relevant to everyone involved these and many other activities, since they all require imagination.

If you were fortunate and were encouraged to play imaginatively early in life, and then continued to use the creative skills you had learned, you are likely to have a good imagination as an adult. Nevertheless, you could still benefit from developing your skills further by learning additional ways of helping good ideas emerge.

Alternatively, you may not have been so lucky and might feel that your imaginative skills are more limited. In that case you would certainly benefit from learning more about how to imagine. While I'm not suggesting you will readily transform yourself into a highly imaginative person, you could certainly benefit from learning how to be better at finding good ideas.

In either case, there will be ways of thinking and approaches to finding ideas which you may not have come across before. You could raise your level of imaginative skill by learning and using these often enough for them to become habits of thought.

In whatever way you view your imaginative skills, you must be born with an imagination since, as evidence I quote in the next chapter shows, you use it from at least from the time of your birth to try to make sense of the mass of new experiences you encounter. Then, from early childhood, you will have begun to play imaginatively, since almost all infants do even if they are not encouraged.

Once you learned to talk, you will have held spoken dialogues with yourself as you imagined in your play. If you were lucky you will have been encouraged in your imaginative play and activities as you progressed through childhood and adolescence. You are then likely to have grown to be an imaginative adult. That is as it should be.

Sadly, infants are not always encouraged in their imaginative play. In school, educational systems too often give insufficient priority to developing imaginative skills, and may focus instead on teaching 'knowledge' thought to be of practical use or helpful in future employment. Educational policies of this type don't take account of the research evidence, published from the time of the 1920s psychologists Lev Vygotsky (1) and Jean Piaget (2) right up to the present time, that children are active in imagining and building their own understandings of the world. This is what 'learning' really amounts to and it is how both children and adults learn, through imaginative responses to the stimuli they encounter.

Kathy Hirsh-Pasek and Roberta Michnick Golinkoff presented this view, supported by with a mass of evidence, in their book with the striking title of *Einstein Never Used Flashcards*. They explained that the view that, to make good progress, children need to focus on learning 'knowledge' from an early age is '… at complete odds…' (3 p. xiii) with the scientific evidence. They argued instead, as their subtitle proclaims, that children '… need to play more and memorise less'. Einstein's parents, they report, encouraged him to play as a child (3 p. 245).

Learning, the evidence has long shown, takes place most effectively by encouraging an imaginative response to experiences rather than by learning 'facts'. Encouragement of this kind is the most effective way of helping children both to learn and to develop a good imagination. They will then be more likely to be able to continue learning (i.e. imagining their own new knowledge) and adapting imaginatively to new situations throughout their lives.

If priority is not given to encouraging infants and children to play and imagine, this can lead to them growing into adults who feel they lack a good imagination. If you think that this may apply to you to any extent, don't be discouraged, since it is never too late to work on improving your imaginative skills.

Of course, if you start to develop your skills as an adult you may find that your early efforts seem modest to you or to others. This will be because your skills have not developed sufficiently. You should not be discouraged by the limitations of your early efforts since your skills will improve as you study and practise approaches which have been shown to be helpful.

That is my key point. Imaginative ability is not something just given to you. Rather, a good imagination is the result of having learned and practiced the skills required for coming up with ideas. Albert Read, in his recent book *The Imagination Muscle*, quotes Leonardo da Vinci's view that creative thinking is '… a discipline to which attention and time should be devoted …' (4 p. xiii). Accept, like Leonardo that, whatever your starting level, there are skills which you could learn and practice throughout life to further improve your imaginative ability.

The evidence, in fact, is that using the imagination is important to each person's development. Many of the leading researchers in this field contributed to a joint book (5) in which they argued, convincingly it seems to me, that the way people develop is by being creative, that is, imaginative. The implication of their argument is that every-one, whatever their line of work or interests, would benefit from using and developing their imaginative skills throughout their lives.

Importantly, the evidence also shows that imagining does not depend on out-of-the-ordinary abilities. Forty years ago D. N. Perkins published a summary and analysis of a wide range of research on this subject, and I will be quoting him several times. One of his conclusions was that imagining '… is a natural comprehensible extension and orchestration of ordinary everyday abilities …' (6 p. 3). After all, imagining depends on essentially the same processes and skills as those used in remembering. To recall something, you have to bring it to mind, that is, to imagine it.

The fact is also that ideas develop through well-understood mental processes, and you could improve your ability to find good ideas if you understood more about how these work. As James Webb Young, an expert on imagining new adverts, put it in a perhaps extreme way:

> '... the production of ideas is just as definite a process as the production of Fords; that the production of ideas, too, runs on an assembly line; that in this production the mind follows an operative technique which can be learned and controlled ...' (7 p. 6).

The first step in this process, as I will explain fully in Chapter 1, is the formation of memories in response to your experiences. Ideas do not come out of a vacuum, but from the existing contents of your mind, principally these memories. The second step is the re-combination of elements of your memories through the subconscious interaction or dialogue between the memories you have accumulated to form the new connections we think of as ideas. These only appear in your conscious mind (the third step) after your memories have interacted and new links have been built.

Since your imagination depends on memories formed from experiences, your ideas clearly grow through contact with other people and the wider world around you, and so your ideas depend on your contact with the society and environment around you. Your imaginative skills will have grown in this way from early in your life through your evolving ability to respond in trying to make sense of each new experience.

This means that there are four key elements to learning how to imagine more effectively.

- First, you could seek out more and more varied experiences in order to feed your imagination. The greater number and variety of your experiences, the more likely you are to come up with good ideas.

- Second, you could learn new ways of encouraging your memories of these experiences to interact in your subconscious.

- Third, you could learn more ways of helping ideas to then pop into your conscious mind.

—
4

- Fourth, you could develop additional skills for evaluating your ideas in order to improve on your initial thoughts.

Chapter 2 consists of 65 lessons which expand on these elements. Each lesson deals with an imaginative skill or way of thinking and working which you could adopt and develop into a habit of mind. Each is based on research evidence or the advice of people with a track record in imaginative work.

This book draws on my previous book, *The Imagination of Experiences* (8), in which I examined the extensive research on the working of the imagination and on forms of collaboration. That book is available as a hardback, paperback, or e-book.

I'm working on a companion book called *How to Collaborate*. It will draw on a some of the same research since collaboration, when it comes down to it, consists of sharing imaginations. As well, many studies have been published of the contrasting ways in which people work together. The result is that we know a good deal about the several different ways of sharing imaginative work in collaborative projects, and how different forms of collaboration are appropriate in contrasting situations. The forthcoming book will draw on this extensive research, as well as on the research on which the modern understanding of the imagination is based.

I've included references to the research on which my conclusions and suggestions are based. This may come across as a bit academic, but I wanted to show that the arguments and advice are soundly based. You may also want to follow up some of these for further reading.

A good many of the examples I give are from my own field of music, though plenty are not. All I would say is that, in my experience, the imagination appears to work the same way in every field. The arguments and the specific advice I present are, in any case, all based on research which applies universally.

Chapter 1. How the imagination works

The experience of having an idea

You probably find that ideas just pop into your mind without conscious thought. The process by which they are produced might therefore seem a mystery to you, and so you may feel that it would be hard to improve your skills. In fact there is a great deal you could learn from research on how ideas develop, and this could help you in your imaginative work.

It becomes clear that imagining is a comprehensible process if it is compared with what most people call remembering. The reason is that remembering involves using your imagination just as much as coming up with a 'new' idea. It depends on bringing to mind memories of something, that is, imagining it. In fact, we generally recombine a number of memories when we remember, such as different features of a room or different parts of an event.

Coming up with ideas which seem new to you depends on essentially the same process, since new ideas are also produced by recombining elements from your memories. As Webb Young put it '… an idea is nothing more nor less than a new combination of old elements.' (7 p. 15). These 'old elements' are the memories which you make from your experiences. The point is that imagining and remembering both depend on recombining your memories. Put like that, you can see that the imaginative process is quite comprehensible.

Nevertheless, you are still likely to be surprised by the way ideas seem to appear as if from nowhere. People highly skilled in imaginative work commonly report the same experience. They also often say they feel that they themselves played no conscious part in producing the ideas.

To give some examples:

- Beethoven, replying to one of his correspondents, wrote, 'You may ask me where I obtain my ideas. I cannot answer this with any clarity. They come unbidden ...' (9 p. 485).

- Novelist Alan Sillitoe wrote that 'I have to wait for inspiration to come. I'll sit here, looking out of the window or at maps, listening to music and then suddenly I'm off.' (10 p. 5).

- The poet A. E. Housman was quoted as describing how: 'As I went along, thinking of nothing in particular, only looking at things around me and following the progress of the seasons, there would flow into my mind, with sudden and un-accountable emotion, sometimes a line or two of verse, sometimes a whole stanza at once.' (11 p. 8).

- Composer John Taverner described the invention of musical ideas as '... something that comes from deep inside one and takes one by surprise, quite honestly. I'm not aware of any conscious delib-eration while I'm at work.' (12 p. 132).

- Playwright Harold Pinter described how: 'Most of the plays are engendered by a line, a word or an image ... The first line of *The Homecoming* is "What have you done with the scissors?" ... I had no further information.' The line of dialogue just came to him, and he went on from there (13).

You are probably also familiar with the sense that an idea pleases you and feels right, or alternatively that it is somehow 'wrong', or at least, wrong for your current project. Descriptions of this sense of an idea or a course of action just feeling right or wrong can be traced back at least as far as Plato's account of Socrates' speech in his defence at his trial, known as the *Apology*.

Socrates described being driven by an inner voice which led him to teach in the ways considered unacceptable by his accusers. He called this an '... an oracle or sign which comes to me ... a kind of voice.' (14 p. 25). As he described it, the inner voice had two characteristics - he was unable to explain it, but even so felt that he must do what it told him.

The same concept is found in the Judeo-Christian tradition as the '… still small voice' (15 p. 292) through which God is said to have spoken to the prophet Elijah, and which is sometimes interpreted as the voice of conscience. We hear this inner voice, and we then somehow know whether an idea is right, or what it is right to do, even though we may not be able to explain this fully to ourselves.

This sense of rightness was investigated by psychoanalyst and neuropsychologist Mark Solms, who concluded that we decide on actions or ideas on the basis of '… affective feelings' (16 p. 138) which are registered in the mid-brain operating subconsciously, rather than through conscious thought. This is the neurological basis of the sense that something feels right or wrong. It is sometimes called gut feeling, since it seems to come from deep inside rather than from conscious thought.

Again, there are published descriptions of this sense of whether an idea is right or not. To pick out a few:

- Mark Haddon explained that he knows his novels are complete when '… somewhere between versions 15 and 25, something happens. The frisson you get when you read your words back and they seem to have been written by someone or something that is not quite you. A rightness like a heavy oak door clicking softly home on to its latch.' (17 p. 5)

- John Taverner described how he could tell whether changes to his music were needed, saying that 'Yes I can [tell], and not only by looking at the music. It could be by looking at the cat … ' (12 p. 145), and that 'When I'm composing in Greece, to walk along and sit by the sea at night or to look at the landscape somehow tells me whether I've got it right or wrong.' (12 p. 145).

- Harold Pinter is quoted describing the sense of knowing when a play was just right and so finished, saying that 'One day I began to write *Ashes to Ashes*, and another day I knew it was complete.' (18 p. 175).

In this chapter I'll try to explain these two experiences, the arrival of ideas as if from nowhere, and the equally-sudden emergence of a sense of their rightness. It will probably be clear to you, maybe after reflecting, that these are both influenced by your memories and experiences, though they obviously don't reflect these sources directly. The question is not whether your ideas are based on your memories, but *how* the ideas relate to them and *why* they take new forms rather than reflecting experiences more directly.

Just to be clear about one thing before going on, some of the research I quote concerns creativity rather than imagination, and the distinction between the two concepts, if any, is important to my argument. For instance, David Hargreaves, Dorothy Miell, and Raymond Mac-Donald suggested that imagination is about perception, about seeing something potentially new, while creativity concerns doing, about making something which may be new (19 p. 3).

That is a fair point, but I don't see how these two concepts can be separated in practice. Creativity is, after all, impossible without imagination since you would be unable to make anything new without having ideas about the form it should take. Equally, having an idea (imagining) is surely a creative act. There was no idea, then one was made, so where does the distinction lie?

Albert Read takes the same line, and describes creativity as '… the imagination's active counterpart.' (4 p. 3). The two terms seem to me to relate to inseparable activities, not least because imagining usually continues directly and indistinguishably into creating, or at least, imagined creating. For this reason research findings on either are relevant to discussions of both.

The illusion of the lone imagination

One problem in developing a better understanding of how your imagination works is the widely-held view that coming up with ideas is a process which takes place just within the individual mind working in isolation. After all, since ideas seem to appear from nowhere, this could easily mislead you into thinking that your level of imaginative skill is simply given to you. However, that view of the imaginative process is not supported by the evidence.

Instead, research shows that the formation of ideas is stimulated by your experience of contact with the people, society, and environment around you. Every idea you have is the result of the intermingling of memories formed through this external contact. You do not really imagine alone.

However, the idea that imagination is an individual process, and that some people just have a special gift of imaginative ability, has a powerful hold on popular understandings. For this reason it may help you gain a better grasp of how the imagination actually works if the view that it is individual process is, so to speak, cleared it out of the way before I go on to give a more accurate account of its operation.

The first thing to take on board is that this view of the imagination is, historically, of relatively recent origin. In his study of how the concept of the imagination has changed through history, J.M. Cocking explained that philosophers in the ancient world, such as Plato, had no conception of the unconscious mind. Plato therefore didn't see ideas as coming from mental processes, and assumed they must be given by the Gods (20 p. 269).

As Cocking went on to explain, the view that ideas came from the human imagination is first found in the writing of medieval Muslim thinkers (20 p. 138). It developed further in Renaissance Europe (20 p. 271) and, as Andy Hamilton described, writers at that time began to describe the visual arts as just that, arts rather than crafts (21 p. 66), reflecting the developing view of the human imagination as the source of art.

The idea reached its zenith in the Romantic era, when artists came to see themselves as creating enduring works, rather than as craftspeople producing pieces more or less to order. That was two hundred years ago, and our understanding of the mental process involved has developed a long way since.

The evidence against this idea

The two key elements of the modern understanding of our imaginative process are that:

- The development of ideas depends on contributions by many people. The evidence does not support the view that individual people working alone are the source of ideas. Social interaction is inherent and normal in imaginative work.

- Even when someone works physically alone, they will still be imagining within the context of traditions, established approaches, and memories made from experiences which took place within their societies. There is no escape from being influenced in this way. Imagining free from the influence of the society around is not possible.

On the first point, Howard Becker found in his study of how a wide variety of art was made that, in every case, the creative work depended on many people rather than just a lone artist (22). He proposed the term *art world* for this constellation of people who contribute to any piece of art.

The same is true in every other field. For instance, a manager imagining a way forward for a company will be influenced by how other people have made such plans in the past, and by consideration of customers and employees. A doctor making a diagnosis (which requires sympathetic imagination) will be influenced by their training, by feedback from colleagues, and by the individual patient.

Distributed creativity has been suggested by both Keith Sawyer and Stacy DeZutter (23) and Eric F. Clarke and Mark Doffman (24) as a term for this same feature of the way ideas emerge. Like Becker, both of these research teams summarised evidence from many studies and found that people doing imaginative work always depended directly on contributions made by (*distributed* between) several people, as well as being indirectly influenced by many more people, past and present.

Imaginative work, the evidence shows, always depends in this way on human interconnectedness and interaction. As the psychologists Steven Sloman and Philip Fernbach put it, 'When you put it all together, human thought is incredibly impressive. But it is a product of community, not of the individual alone.' (25 p. 5). So, my first point is that ideas are never produced just by one person imagining alone. Rather, everyone doing imaginative work depends on direct and indirect contributions by many other people.

Turning to the second point, even if several people contribute to the evolution of each idea, there must of course still be an individual part of the process. As Adam Lindon and Eric F. Clarke put it, '… cognition must originate in the mind of the individual (after all, our thoughts, insights and new discoveries seem to occur in our own heads)…' (26 p. 54). The point is, though, that this process of individual thinking and imagining does not take place in isolation from the surrounding society.

As Sawyer put it in another contribution to the debate, 'all creativity … involves social groups of individuals' (27 p. 19) since the process of one person having an idea consists of the interaction in their mind of ideas and memories formed within the society around them. He went on to describe how new ideas emerge through a process involving '… a social group of individuals engaged in complex, unpredictable interactions. It is the entire system that creates, not the individual alone.' (27 p. 19).

His point is that both each person's memories, and the way they recombine to form new ideas, are the result of social interaction rather than being the product only of their individual minds.

To give a detailed example, Mozart has often been seen as an example of the autonomous genius conjuring up brilliant music just from within his own mind. However, the style of his music and his fluency in composition were not the result just of innate talent, but developed within the context of his intensely musical family background and his hot-housing as a child prodigy and young adult touring Europe.

As a result he had a detailed familiarity with late eighteenth-century musical idioms, particularly Italian opera and sacred music, and the music written in the relatively recently-developed styles of the Classical era (roughly 1750-1820) more generally. Music in the style of the Mannheim school was a particularly important influence. He was clearly not just an individual composing in isolation from the surrounding social and musical environment.

The evidence is also that he was also deeply involved in contemporaneous thinking and social movements. As Nicholas Till described in his book *Mozart and the Enlightenment* (28), his music was influenced not only by living in the period when the ideas of the eighteenth-century Enlightenment were dominant, but also by Freemasonry and its values. Till described the arrival of Freemasonry in Vienna, the increasing involvement in the movement of progressive aristocrats and bourgeois like Mozart, and Mozart's eventual decision to join a lodge of specifically Catholic masons (28 pp. 117-129). He linked changes in Mozart's music to the evolution of his attitudes within this context.

In spite of all the accumulated evidence, there are still claims that people like Mozart simply have the gift of an exceptional imagination, and could produce complex work with little apparent effort. For instance, there are written accounts claimed to be by Mozart and others describing hearing music complete in their heads and then just writing it down, and these have been used to support the idea of the genius creator imagining alone. However, these accounts have in fact been shown to be forgeries created to support the idea of the lone genius (29 pp. 96-108).

The reality is that the great composers had to labour long and hard when imagining. For instance, Beethoven made more than two hundred sketches before he found what he felt was exactly the right version of his *Ode to Joy* (30 p. 148). The evidence is that this 'genius' composer not only needed to work hard on writing his music in this way, but also that both his initial ideas and the final form of his pieces were influenced by the culture and traditions current at their time.

In this case he was clearly influenced by the values reflected in the poem by Schiller which he was setting, and by the intellectual and aesthetic climate within which both he and Schiller were working. As Sheryl Fontaine and Susan Hunter argued, the writer, and by implication anyone else doing imaginative work, never '… writes alone.' (31 p. xxiii).

Why the idea persists

I hope that I have said enough to show that the view that ideas are produced just through one person's mental activity does not fit the evidence. The question, though, is why this idea persists, as it certainly does in Western Art (= Classical) Music, even though it is an historically recent idea and has little basis in fact.

As I mentioned above, one reason is that the mental processes which lead to ideas suddenly popping into consciousness can give the misleading impression that ideas come just from within our own minds. Neuroscientists John Kounios and Mark Beeman examined the evidence of how this illusion is created.

In their study of the brain activity which takes place before and when an idea arrives, they showed that brain areas associated with subconscious thought light up first, followed by areas associated with conscious thought at the moment when the person becomes aware of an idea (32 p. 86). Decisions are made within our brains, as Benjamin Libert also showed in his earlier research, before we become aware of them, not at the start of conscious thinking (33 pp. 42 & 96-7).

Commenting on Libert's findings, Moheb Costandi describeed how:

> When selecting between different courses of action, the brain weighs up the options available, with different groups of neurons gathering information about each possible course of action. When one of these groups accumulates enough evidence, its activity level passes a threshold, and the commands for movements associated with that particular course of action are issued. (34 p. 99)

This is a revealing description of the neurological activity which lies behind the subconscious process through which we come up with ideas or make decisions. Each notion emerges, not through concentrated thought, but from a flux of subconscious alternatives and possibilities. When one of these becomes sufficiently well-formed it appears in our conscious mind as an idea or a decision.

The result can be that a person may think that they have just come up with an idea when, unknown to them, it had already been developing in their subconscious through the exploration of many possibilities. As Kounios and Beeman explained '... the aha moment [when we have an idea] occurs when an idea that's already slightly activated in the right hemisphere [of the brain] – but is still unconscious – suddenly emerges into awareness as an insight.' (32 p. 80).

Psychologist Vladimir Konečni drew the same conclusion from his review of a wide range of experiences of imagining, and quoted similar studies showing spikes in brain activity prior to an insight (30 p. 144). The point is that, rather than appearing as if from nowhere, ideas emerge into our conscious minds after a period of subconscious rumination.

Since we are unaware of this subconscious process, we may be misled into thinking we have found an idea just at the moment when it occurs to us consciously. While we could assume, like Plato, that the explanation for this is that ideas come from an external source, nowadays people are more likely to think that they come just from within their own minds, from their own personal source of 'inspiration'. As Kounios and Beeman put it, this can mislead people into thinking that 'If it [an idea] came all of a sudden, then it must be my idea!' (32 p. 104).

As I explained in the previous section, the evidence from studies of people imagining is that their ideas do not arise just in their minds working in isolation, but instead that the process depends on memories formed in response to the stimulus of interaction with the people and the environment around them. An idea is never just 'your idea'. Any idea or solution to a problem which appears in your conscious mind will have matured in your subconscious through the inter-action of elements of the memories you have accumulated through your of social and environmental experiences.

From this discussion, you may already be able to see that, rather than being mysterious, the imagination operates on the basis of a set of well-understood processes or 'mechanics' which I'll go on to describe in the rest of the chapter. The implication of this understanding of how we come up with ideas is that you could improve the working of the processes involved in your imagination by learning new ways of helping them to operate more effectively.

Three features of the imagination

To return to the point made at the start, imagining and remembering are closely related or even, perhaps, aspects of the same form of mental activity. In his study of the human capacity to imagine, Jim Davies described imagination as '... the creation of ideas in your head ...' (35 p. 1). He included in this the mental process usually described as remembering, such as calling to mind the image of a pot of jam or, as he put it, peanut butter.

While remembering certainly requires the use of the imagination to bring memories to mind, this book is concerned with imagination in the narrower sense of having ideas which are somehow 'new'. However, Davies' broad view of this human ability does help to underline a key point about the process of coming up with ideas – that the imagination depends on having memories formed through experiences.

Remembering a pot of jam depends on having seen a pot of jam. Importantly, when we remember a specific pot of jam, we re-combine our memories (experiences) of the pot of jam, and to some extent at least we imagine (remember) a composite pot. One result is the common experience in remembering an object, event, or place and later finding that we have recalled some details incorrectly.

In his book *The Imaginary*, the philosopher Jean-Paul Sartre described remembering a building in St. Etienne but noted that his recollections of that building were 'contaminated' by memories of a building in Paris (36 p. 91). That is the nature of remembering: that we recall composite memories which are in effect newly created ideas. As Davies put it, 'The elements of your imagination come from your memory. Indeed, where else could they come from?' (35 p. 254).

Remembering and imagining therefore both depend on re-combining memories, but the difference between them as the terms are normally understood is that remembering involves calling to mind memories of a specific person or thing, whereas imagining depends on the often unexpected or unexplained recombination of memories to produce ideas which seem new to us.

This concept of recombination is the key idea put forward by novelist Arthur Koestler in his book on the creative imagination. He called this 'bisociation', which he defined as '... the discovery of hidden similarities ...' (37 p. 27). Koestler's point was that the process of coming up with creative ideas, that is, ideas which are in some way new at least to the person concerned, depends on building links between previously unconnected memories.

He saw the creative processes in comedy, science, and the arts as essentially the same, and as one of producing jokes, making scientific breakthroughs, or producing art through building connections between elements of experience and knowledge which were not previously seen as linked. As Steve Jobs put it, '... creativity is just connecting things ...' (38).

This view, that imagination is based on making new connections, was also put forward by Read, who quoted the poet T.S. Eliot describing imagining as '...connecting previously unconnected matrices of experience ...' (4 p. 28). Like Koestler, Read saw the imaginative process in the arts and the sciences as essentially the same. He quoted scientists who used terms similar to those used by artists in describing how they imagined (4 pp. 77-8), and noted that many leading scientists were also active in the arts (4 pp. 78-9). Einstein was, as you may know, a keen violinist.

Ideas, therefore, do not come straight from the body of memories we have formed. If they did, they would reflect those memories more directly, even replicating them exactly. The process is clearly more complex, and has three main features.

Accumulating memories

The first of these concerns the way in which we make memories. The specific ways in which this takes place are the reason why your imaginative ability is not fixed but is open to improvement, not least through expanding and adding variety to your range of experiences.

This will lead to changes in the way your brain works since additional neuronal connections are built up as we have new experiences. As Costandi noted '... our brain modifies its structure and functions continuously in response to every experience we have.' (34 p. 58). It will help in developing your imaginative skills if you understand more about how this happens.

Until the mid-twentieth century the structure of the brain was seen as fixed. However, evidence began to emerge, initially in a study by a team led by Marian Diamond (39) which showed that the number of neural connections was higher among rats which had lived in a stimulating environment than among those which had lacked stimulation. Susan Magsamen and Ivy Ross quoted Diamond's findings in their book on the effect of art on the brain, and explained that changes in the brain's wiring are most likely to occur as a result of stimuli which are both salient and important to you (40 p. 13).

It is normal for the number of neural connections to increase rapidly in young children since they encounter many new experiences. If too few connections form early on due to a lack of stimulation this can lead to lower mental ability later, as Lisa Feldman Barrett showed in her study (42 p. 50). Early stimulation and a variety of experiences help equip people with the plentiful neural connections required for good imaginative skills. These plentiful connections are crucial due to the process which Sahakian is quoted as describing whereby, as you grow up and '... the brain is getting more efficient, you get rid of extra synapses [connections between brain cells] you don't want.' (41 p. 10).

However, the type as well as the amount of stimulation you receive as a child can affect the likelihood of growing to be an imaginative adult. As I mentioned earlier, Hirsh-Pasek and Michnick Golinkoff presented extensive evidence contrary to the view that children's academic development will benefit if their parents prioritise formal educational experiences for their children when young (3).

They refer to a study that showed that children who received more 'academic' teaching in preschool were no better at academic tasks later than children who mainly played at preschool, but the latter were more creative (3 p. 12). Children's minds stray more widely in play than in organised 'learning', and so the playing child is more likely to develop the wide-ranging brain connections needed for good imaginative skills than the child who has a more regimented regime of 'learning'.

The lesson for adults wishing to develop their imaginative skills is they should try to re-learn how to behave in more childlike ways: to play with ideas and possibilities, to let their focus stray widely, to flit from one thing to another, and above all to expose themselves to a wide variety of new experiences in the way children do as they grow. Habits of behaviour such as these can help build and reinforce new brain connections.

Once you've taken on board that your imaginative skills will grow as you widen your range of experiences, it is then important to bear in mind exactly how experiences are recorded as memories. There are four separate features of the process by which we accumulate memories from our engagement in the world around us:

1. We actively shape our perception of new stimuli in the light of memories formed earlier.
2. This includes the shaping of memory formation by concepts and ideas which we have absorbed.
3. Our memories are formed in a social environment.
4. We are selective about the experiences we register.

First, our accumulated memories help shape how we experience the world. As Jonathan Webber explained in his introduction to the Sartre book mentioned earlier, Sartre's argument is based on a fundamental distinction between 'the matter of an experience and its form' (43 p. xiii). The 'matter' of experience is, for instance, an object such as a house. The 'form' of experience concerns how we perceive the house, which in turn is affected by our previous experiences of houses.

On this theme, a team led by Marte Otten investigated the reliability of memory, and wrote in the Abstract to their paper that '... memories can be shaped to fit our expectations, which can generate false memories.' (44). In their own experiments they found that even short-term memories were distorted fairly quickly as the participants 'corrected' their recollection of things they had seen to fit with their perception of what they thought they should have seen.

Evidence such as this shows that our memories result from the inescapable fact that we bring our existing perceptions to bear on the way we see any new experience. As a result, our memories are not exact images of the original experiences. As Solms explained, supporting his argument with a mass of evidence, 'Perception proceeds *from the inside outwards*, always from the viewpoint of the subject.' (16 pp. 184-5). We create, or imagine, an understanding of the events and things we encounter, rather than remembering them exactly, and we develop these understandings in the light of our previous experiences.

New memories formed in this way will, in turn, affect how you experience further stimuli. By seeking out a wider variety of experiences, you will reshape the way you perceive further experiences due to the formation of additional neural connections in your brain as each new memory is formed. This will help widen the range of your imaginative ability.

On the **second** point, Alison Hills and Alexander Bird explained that we do not imagine in an unconstrained way, but we are '... guided by models and constraints ...' (45 p. 8) as well as our own previously-formed memories. This is certainly true in the arts since, as philosopher Noël Carroll pointed out, artists depend on the traditions they have inherited, a dependence which is not consistent with the idea of '... godlike individualism ...' (46 p. 211), which is the essence of the idea of the creative genius.

Björn Merker made this same argument, describing creativity in music not as something that takes place in isolation, but as occupying '... the crest of a historical travelling wave of gradual change and diversification ...' (47 p. 36) since all innovations draw and build on existing ideas, styles, and approaches.

That is the real meaning of originality, starting with things as they are and taking some steps away rather than thinking you have invented something wholly new. Ideas completely detached from existing ideas or earlier practice are not really possible because we inescapably draw on our memories when imagining, and these include our familiarity with existing ideas.

Again, encountering and digesting new models and concepts will help reshape how you form memories. A well-known example is the encounter of European artists with African and other non-European art at the start of the 'modern' era prior to World War I, and the changes to which this led in their own art.

The **third** point, on social interaction, is that our experiences take place through contact with our environment. Thoughts and ideas come from the memories and learning which we accumulate through social and environmental contact.

This brings me back to the work of Vygotsky, whose research in the early years of the Soviet Union focused on the way children learn. He found that children learned principally through interaction with others, rather than being passive recipients of knowledge taught to them, and that they learned through their own imaginative reactions to their experiences of this contact (1 p. 20). As Sawyer put it, '… the child constructs knowledge through socially situated action.' (48 p. 8).

This inescapably social nature of the learning process is the reason why infants learn to speak most effectively, as Alex Beard described, through being spoken to rather than from passively overhearing speech (49 p. 61). This is reflected in the recent research finding by John Spencer's team that infants' brains change more rapidly the more they are spoken to (50). The social stimulus of the interaction provokes the development of the neural connections which the child then uses in imagining how to respond. They then imitate and try to speak, not always making sense at first.

As an example, Patricia Kuhl found that, when various methods of teaching Chinese to Western children were tested, the only children who learned anything were those spoken to in Chinese (51). The interaction with the other person provoked the children to imagine their own knowledge, that is, how to speak some Chinese.

For a child, imagining new knowledge in response to the stimulus of social interaction is a form of imaginative play, and it is this imaginative play which eventually becomes the basis of the adult creative imagination. As Seana Moran and Vera John-Steiner concluded from their review of Vygotsky's research, '…the origins of creative imagination [lie in] children's symbolic play.' (52 p. 71.

As Sigmund Freud also noted, '… every child at play behaves like a creative writer, in that he creates a world of his own.' (53 p. 437). Girls do this too! Children, play, create, and learn through using their imaginations. Throughout the rest of our lives we continue to make memories and ideas which are new to us from the stimulus of social interaction, even though we don't usually think of this as play. We imagine our responses to these interactions before or as we react, or sometimes by imagining alternative responses after reacting. In this way we create our own new knowledge.

The **fourth** point is that we select how we engage with our environment, rather than simply encountering and absorbing experiences or information. As a result of our active participation in making our memories, we select some stimuli or some aspects of an experience rather than others, or some more than others, and engage with those we select.

Neuroscientist György Buzsáki (54) explained that the brain is not like a computer, accepting all the data fed into it. Rather, as soon a child is born, their brain is clearly working on the basis of structures and quasi-understandings which are already there. As neurologist Antonio Damasio also explained, 'At birth, the human brain comes to development endowed with drives and instincts …' (55 p. 126).

From the very start of our lives, we don't just passively absorb information and experiences, with knowledge accumulated as a result. Rather, as we are stimulated by our contact with the world around us, we refer to the mental structures and memories we already possess and subconsciously select how to create our own new understandings.

Also, the process of forming memories is not a detached or intellectual one, as is clear from the way infants start to build their own understandings immediately from birth. This view that knowledge and ideas arise from affect and emotion has also been traced back to Vygotsky by Mahn and John-Steiner (56 p. 47). The evidence from Vygotsky's and later studies is that experiencing and imagining, as well as depending on our active engagement with other people and the environment, always involves our emotions and feelings. As Paul Noordhof put it, this '... involves *the sensuous imagination (through simulation) of an emotion-guided process* ...' (57 p. 337).

The fact is, we perceive by sensing rather than by analysing our environment. As Damasio showed in his later book on human perception and development (58), we experience our environment by sensing, as do all animals. These senses provoke feelings which lead us to create (imagine) our understandings, that is, to learn. Both external stimulation and an internal imaginative response are necessary for this process of learning and the accumulation of the memories from which ideas are formed.

Ideas, then, arise from memories formed from experiences, and we have a good understanding of the way in which we accumulate experiences through our social and environmental interactions. We must therefore have some control over our imaginative process since we can work to build up a varied fund of memories, and so improve our ability to generate ideas.

As Steve Jobs commented, people good at coming up with ideas have learned how to '... connect experiences they've had and synthesize new things. And the reason they were able to do that was that they've had more experiences or they have thought more about their experiences than other people.' (38).

Jobs was clearly describing skills at which we can improve by adding to our stock of memories and digesting them more thoroughly. In the next chapter I'll describe ways in which we can use this understanding of how we accumulate memories in order to improve our imaginative abilities.

The dialogue between memories

The ideas which come to us clearly do not reflect our memories directly. Rather, they result from the intermingling and recombination of experiences and snippets of experiences. Our many memories interact and reconnect through a form of dialogue, leading to their recombination into the new forms we think of as ideas. This process of subconscious dialogue or interaction is the reason why it is often hard to account for the character of our ideas.

As an example, the writer Martin Crimp, commenting on his own writing to an interviewer, described:

> ... a figure balefully called 'The Writer'. The Writer smashes up the narrator's house, ruins his piano, steals his electric toothbrush. Worst of all are the things he writes. 'How can someone who spends so many hours watching trees change colour, or children skipping, come up with all that pain and brutality?' (59 p. 15)

Whilst Crimp could not account for the words he wrote, he still recognised that they came from within himself somehow. We all, like Crimp, lack conscious control over our internal dialogue but, as he found, it can be highly and surprisingly productive.

The use of the term 'dialogue' for this process of the recombination of memories and building of new connections comes from the work of Mikhail Bakhtin (60), who analysed the way novels depend for their richness on dialogues or encounters between the contrasting characters and the different worlds each brings into a novel. His concept of dialogue between the experiences of a variety of characters and worlds of experience is widely used nowadays to describe the way ideas develop through interaction between our various memories.[1]

---

[1] For instance, the term 'dialogue' was used in this way by Fernyhough (65), Fontaine and Hunter (31; 51), Glazner (140), and Shepherd (141.

This idea of an internal dialogue has been connected with the view of William James, described by Costandi as 'the father of modern psychology' (34 p. 21), who argued that personality is multiple rather than singular, with each person not a simple self but the focus of a complex set of inter-relationships (61 p. 291).

The two ideas of dialogue and of our many-sided personalities were brought together by psychologists Hubert Hermans and Harry Kempen (62) in the concept of the dialogic self, in which a person is seen not as a single self but as consisting of a dialogue between many elements. They argued that human behaviour is based on this interaction and dialogue, and described a person's identity as inseparable from other people, and engaged in a continuous process of social dialogue, writing that:

> Since the *Me* is also a 'social *Me*', they [people] are not able to think, feel, or act in isolation from the community in which they participate. They are continuously involved in dialogues ... (62 p. 72)

Since the elements which enter into the dialogue within each person are the result of contact between them and the world around, the dialogue itself clearly operates within a social context. This socially situated internal dialogue is the source of our ideas, not simply our individual minds working in isolation.

It is now widely accepted that it is this dialogue between our memories or experiences which leads to the sudden appearance of ideas in our minds of ideas whose character may be hard to explain even to ourselves. Our ideas seem new, and often unexpected, to us because they are based on fresh re-combinations of elements of our memories. As Einstein was quoted as explaining, '... combinatory play seems to be the essential feature in productive thought.' (63 p. 142). Without this internal process of play, dialogue, or recombination of memories, we would have no new ideas.

In the next chapter, after setting out advice on feeding your internal dialogue with more experiences, I will describe ways of helping this subconscious dialogue operate more freely. Adopting these approaches, if you don't already use them, could help you to find more, and more promising, ideas.

Subconscious rumination

This process of recombining elements of our knowledge and experience to form new ideas takes place largely in our subconscious minds. The result is that we don't control the shape our ideas take. While we can choose to prepare by feeding our subconscious with experiences, or by thinking around a problem or task, we cannot control what our imagination will produce.

This is not only due to the process being subconscious, but also because it can operate in a seemingly chaotic way, often leading to ideas which may surprise us. For instance, the mathematician Henri Poincaré described the disorderly nature of his subconscious process, a disorder which he saw as an essential part of imagining. He is quoted as describing an experience of how:

> Ideas rose in crowds; I felt them collide until pairs interlocked, so to speak, making a stable combination. Only certain ones are harmonious, and, consequently, are at once useful and beautiful ... Only this disorder itself permits unexpected combination. (64 p. 36)

The view that the dialogue between memories is subconscious was examined by psychologist Charles Fernyhough (65), who noted how young children discuss with themselves what they are doing as they play. He explained that this way of thinking in dialogues becomes internalised and subconscious as we grow up. In his study of this inner voice from which ideas come to us he found that, among the people he studied '… the mysteries of inner speech become more comprehensible when we recognise that it has the properties of a dialogue.' (65 p. 15).

In their parallel study, Moran and John-Steiner also argued that childhood play is the origin of the creative imagination because 'Once play is internalized, it forms the basis of fantasy, which develops further when linked to inner speech.' (52 p. 71).

Since it is this dialogue, operating subconsciously, which leads to ideas and solutions to problems appearing in our conscious minds, these often seem to emerge more readily when we are relaxed or distracted. The conscious mind is then less active, or even inactive as when we are asleep.

As Konečni noted: 'Once an impasse is reached, relaxation and letting the mind wander are helpful ...' (30 pp. 143-4). This research finding is reflected by the fact that many descriptions of the arrival of ideas include mention of being distracted by walking, travelling, sleeping, or taking a break. To give a few examples from my own field of music:

- Paul McCartney described how he found the melody for the song *Yesterday* in his head when he woke up one day (66). He regularly composed melodies when awake and so his subconscious simply continued while he was asleep.

- Freya Bailes and Laura Bishop described composers solving problems on bicycle rides or walks when stuck for ideas, and the example of Mozart finding that ideas came to him when travelling by carriage or walking (67 p. 70).

- The same researchers quoted the composer Karlheinz Stockhausen recalling '... that very often when I'd worked until late at night, I gave up; the brain continued working on the problem during my sleep, and I knew the solution next morning.' (67 p. 61).

- Accounts of composers such as Beethoven, Mahler, and Britten examined by George Predota (68) include mention of how they liked to take walks, notebook in pocket. They found that musical ideas would occur to them when distracted in this way. He also described how other composers such as Britten, Rossini, and Richard Strauss found that ideas occured to them while taking a break.

It seems clear that, if we stop thinking consciously about a problem and do something else such as walking or resting or, in a sense, turning the conscious mind off by falling asleep, ideas may then start to develop more readily in our subconscious. Of course, we remain unaware that this process of subconscious rumination is taking place, and we will only realise that ideas have been developing during a break when they eventually pop into consciousness.

The other sense which arises from the subconscious imagination is that an idea feels 'right' or 'wrong'. As I mentioned earlier, this sense of 'rightness' is sometimes described as gut feeling. This brings me to the evidence that cognition (understanding) and imagination are embodied, rather than being processes of which take place wholly in the brain.

In the earlier of his books which I quote, entitled *Descartes' Error* (55), Damasio argued that the seventeenth-century philosopher René Descartes was wrong to think that '… the soul by which I am what I am is entirely distinct from the body.' (69 p. 101), that is, that thinking and feeling take place in a 'mind' separate from our bodies. Damasio went on to demonstrate how bodily and 'mental' sensing and thinking are one integrated process.

He described the symptoms of people, including his own patients, who had suffered damage to the parts of the brain which integrate signals from elsewhere in the body with those from other regions of the brain. This damage often left the patients devoid of feelings and unable to make choices.

People with wholly intact brains, Damasio argued, can feel what they want to do and therefore choose, and this is because the ability to do so depends on the integrated interaction of the signals from body with those from the rest of the brain. Solms also described how this subconscious process of brain-body sensing eventually leads to conscious feelings, and so to the awareness both of ideas and the sense that they are 'right' or 'wrong' (16 p. 99).

This finding could explain why we experience both the sudden appearance of ideas, and a sense of their rightness, as coming from somewhere other than our conscious minds. We experience this because they both result from the integrated working of the brain-body system. This also explains why we can both imagine and choose without fully understanding the basis on which we do so.

This concept of the subconscious dialogue is closely related to the mode of operation of our mental processes known as the default state. Experimental psychologist Ethan Kross described this state as one in which we decouple from the present moment, and noted that most people do this for about a third of the time. We are then transported to a review of '… past events, imagined scenarios, and other internal musings.' (70 p. xx) over which we have limited control. The brain defaults to this activity when not '… otherwise engaged …' (70 p. xx).

The processes of reminiscence and reverie which take place when the mind is in its default state enable us, as Kross put it, to satisfy '… the inescapable need we all have to use our minds to make sense of experience …' (70 p. 9), to enable us to evaluate experiences and ideas (70 p. 12), and to run mental simulations and explore possibilities (70 p. 13). These are the means by which we begin to make new connections, find patterns and explanations, and so come up with ideas or perspectives which seem new to us. They are the very activities which I've described as taking place in through a subconscious dialogue.

The existence and nature of the subconscious mind are well established and fairly well understood due to the wide range of research I've summarised in this section. While cause and effect between neurological activity and thinking processes are hard to demonstrate, the evidence does suggest that we experience the sudden appearance of ideas as if from nowhere because their development depends on the integrated body-brain process which underlie the default state. This seems to me probably why we are likely to feel that our imaginations reside in our subconscious minds.

Once again, I'll set out in Chapter 2 ways of making more effective use of these subconscious processes in order to generate ideas.

Conclusion

If the view I've put forward is correct, it must be impossible for anyone to fully understand their own imaginative process, since much of it is subconscious. As Solms noted,

'... *we are unaware of most of what we perceive and learn ...*' (16 p. 78). There is a risk that this lack of awareness could lead you to think that ideas come just from your own mind working in isolation, and that the quality of your ideas depends mainly on your inherent imaginative ability.

There is no justification for this. Even though you may feel you don't understand how your own imagination works, that doesn't mean that the imaginative process can't be understood.

Even if you were lucky enough to have been stimulated and encouraged to use your imagination from an early age, and so maybe feel that you are naturally imaginative, your level of imaginative ability is the result of the encouragement you received and the extent to which you then built on your early imaginative skills. It is not innate. In fact, everyone with a normal brain has an imagination and is also capable of improving their imaginative skills.

In the next chapter I will describe many ideas and techniques which could help you to produce and evaluate ideas more effectively, whatever your starting level. If you learn these and apply them as you work they will gradually become habits of mind which you will then use automatically as you imagine.

Chapter 2. Lessons to help you imagine

The 'mechanics' of how the imagination operates, as you will have seen in Chapter 1, are fairly well understood, and we also know that it relies on mental abilities you use regularly in other activities. To imagine, you only need a range of experiences and memories, a subconscious mind, and other normal human attributes. That's why I'm confident that the advice in this chapter, covering a wide variety of thinking processes for use when imagining, could help you improve your skills beyond their current level.

The point is that 'Creativity depends on how people think', as Steven Smith, Thomas Ward and Ronald Finke put it in their book in which they analysed creative thinking processes (71 p. 1), so learning new habits of thought is likely to help you in your search for good ideas.

As an example, back in the 1930s Joseph Rossman carried out a study of hundreds of inventors, and found that there were distinctive aspects to how they thought. Principally, they had an '... emotional reaction to needs which they experience and [an] openness of neural connections in their brains.' (72 p. 87). That is, they let their feelings become engaged as they imagined, and were open to making connections between things which might not have previously been seen as linked.

My argument is that anyone, whether or not they see themselves as imaginative or carry out work traditionally seen as creative, can learn and practice ways of thinking such as these in order to improve their skills. This improved imaginative ability will be helpful in many every-day, as well as 'creative', activities.

For this reason, my objectives differ from those of Julia Cameron in her widely-read book *The Artist's Way* (73). While her book contains many good suggestions, her focus is on ways of overcome artistic blocks, and not all her advice comes across as readily applicable by people engaged in activities other than the arts.

More importantly in some ways, she presented creativity as a spiritual process, with ideas coming from a source she called the 'Great Creator' (73 p. xiv). Without wishing to become embroiled in theological arguments, the point is that imagining and creating are not mysterious processes, and so there is no need to think, like Plato, that ideas come from somewhere outside ourselves. In fact, if you think of ideas as just 'given' to you, this might this might lead you to dismiss the potential which everyone has for improving their imaginative skills.

Rather than needing to wait for inspiration, divine or otherwise, the evidence is instead that you can actively intervene to help the your imaginative process along. As Sidney Parnes and his team reported forty-five years ago in their *Guide To Creative Action*, '... research over the last twenty-five years has made it increasingly clear the there are many processes a person can use to help increase the *likelihood* that the chance connection [i.e. inspiration] will take place.' (74 p. 14).

A great deal of evidence supporting the view of Parnes' team view has accumulated since their book came out, and there are now known to be many techniques and skills you could learn and apply to increase your chances of coming up with good ideas. Take this basic point on board, and then study and learn from the wide range of research findings and advice on imaginative skills which I've assembled here.

Remember also that your ideas result from well-understood mental processes used as a matter of course. You are clearly capable of learning how to apply these more effectively and so imagine better than you do at present. Regularly using these newly-acquired skills will help turn them into habits of thought which you then do not need to apply consciously.

Widening your range of experiences

LESSON 1. Experience is the food of the imagination. The Roman poet Lucretius, drawing on a long philosophical tradition, wrote that 'Nothing can come from nothing.' (75). His words were quoted by George Mandler, whose argument, like Lucretius, was that new ideas do not come from out of the blue, from nothing, even if this can seem to you to be the case when they pop into your mind. He described how they arise instead from '... everyday processes of the human mind and body.' (76 p. 9).

Literary critics William Wimsatt and Munroe Beardsley commented on this process of ideas arising from life, describing how, in poetry 'There is a gross body of sensory and mental experience, which lies behind and in some way causes every poem.' (11 pp. 479-80).

So, lesson one is that, to imagine, you need this body of memories formed through experiences. While this might seem obvious, it has important implications, and in particular it means that improving your imaginative ability begins with working on your range of experiences.

LESSON 2. Have more experiences. Since ideas come from your memories, your imaginative ability will improve if you accumulate more, and more varied, memories through having more, and more diverse, experiences. The great fund of memories we all develop was described by philosopher Roland Barthes as an '... immense dictionary ...' (77 p. 147) on which the imagination draws. The key point to take on board is that the wider the variety of memories you have accumulated, the better your ideas are likely to be.

Julia Cameron emphasised the importance of this search for more experiences, calling it 'Stocking the Pond' (73 p. 21). The ceramic artist Carolyn Genders, for example, described how she constantly seeks out additional visual images. These accumulate in her memory over time, and she reports how '... sometimes an idea germinates in my mind surfacing years later.' (78 p. 3). She gave examples of other artists who follow the same approach.

I quoted Barrett in Chapter 1 on the finding that new connections are formed in our brains in response to exper-iences (42 p. 50). The point is that seeking out new and more varied experiences will lead to the development of add-itional connections in your brain, changes in the way your brain works, and so to improvements in your imaginative skills. As playwright Anton Chekhov put it, 'If you want to work on your art, work on your life.' (79).

LESSON 3. Seek experiences actively. You should not just accumulate experiences passively. As I explained in the previous chapter, the evidence supports Damasio's view that ideas arise from '… the interactions between individuals and environment …' (80 p. 59), so actively seek out more, and more varied, experiences. Specifically, make sure you engage in the society, the arts, activities, debates, and conflicts around you. I quoted Magsamen and Ross's evidence earlier showing that intense experiences will have the greatest effect in building new links within your brain (40 p. 13), so seek them out.

As an example, the Nobel Prize-winning Chilean poet Pablo Neruda had an busy life as a writer, diplomat, elected politician, world traveller, and as a participant in important events in twentieth-century history. His autobiography is called *I confess that I have lived* (81). If you can say the same, then you possess a key ingredient needed for a good imagination – memories of many and varied experiences, and of profound experiences in particular.

LESSON 4. Try to be curious, open to varied experiences, and tolerate ambiguity. These are some of the characteristics of imaginative people identified by Anne Roe in her study of personality types and their relationship to forms of employment (82). She also referred to creative people's preference for complexity and heightened perception.

Some of you may feel you've already developed these characteristics, and if so, you should cherish and develop them. If you feel you don't yet match these descriptions, try to change your usual behaviour. Try, for example, to avoid deciding how you feel about a new experience until you've sensed its full complexity, rather than settling too rapidly on one reaction or another. Allow your feelings to resolve in your imagination as and when you have inwardly digested the experience.

LESSON 5. Engage in different cultures. Research shows that people's imaginative ability is likely to be greater if they have lived and participated in cultures other than their own. That may mean the culture of another country or of a contrasting group in their own country. The point, though, is not just to travel, but to engage actively in the different culture.

Chi-yue Chiu and Angela Kay-y Leung found in their research that multi-cultural experiences can '... liberate people from their mental sets by providing intellectual materials and opportunities ... [that] foster the development of the cognitive skills that give rise to creative performance ... [and] increase people's receptiveness to ideas from other cultures.' (83 p. 3).

William Maddux and Adam Galinsky came to the same conclusion in their research, but also described how the extent to which people benefited depended on the '... degree to which individuals had adapted to different cultures' (84 Abstract). In a separate study, another team of Leung's also found that a substantial effect on creativity depended '... on the extent to which individuals open themselves to foreign culture.' (85 p. 169).

Engaging actively in another culture appears to be one of the most effective ways of exposing yourself to influences and experiences which you would not otherwise encounter. So, take up opportunities to live in another country or to engage in a different part of your own society, but make sure you engage actively, make friends there, and live the life of that culture.

Activities in the imaginative process

LESSON 6. Having an idea is not a one-step process. Imagining has been thought of as having several stages since at least the time of ancient Sanskrit scholars. Mark Reybrouck described the four stages they identified as: first emptiness and undefined elements, then preverbal grasping of thoughts, next mental verbalisation, and finally expression (86 p. 53).

The best-known modern proposal along these lines, put forward by Graham Wallas in 1926, is that there are four stages to imagining: **Preparation, Incubation, Illumination, and Verification** (87 p. viii). He based his analysis on accounts of their imaginative processes by eminent scientists and mathematicians. These included the German scientist Herman von Hemholtz, who was quoted by Kounios and Beaman describing the way in which ideas would occur to him:

> It was always necessary, first of all, that I should have turned my problem over on all sides to such an extent that I had all its angles and complexities 'in my head.' ... Then ... there must come an hour of complete physical freshness and quiet well-being, before the good ideas arrived ... they liked especially to make their appearance while I was taking an easy walk over wooded hills in sunny weather. (32 p. 29).

von Helmholtz identified three separate activities here: developing a full understanding of a problem, a period of rest or a relaxed break, and then the arrival of a new idea. Wallas incorporated these into his model and added a fourth, verification, which would take place subsequently. If you want to follow up on similar or alternative ideas on imaginative stages, you will find a review in the endnote.[i]

Having read the many contributions to the debate on this subject, I've come to the conclusion that Wallas' ideas stand up remarkably well, and I'll be using his four terms in this chapter. The key thing you should take on board, though, is that there are several steps involved in imagining, and it is not just a matter of waiting around for ideas to appear.

Since there are separate and definable stages or activities in imagining, you should aim to learn about ways in which you could learn to carry out each of them more effectively. You will then increase the likelihood of finding ideas, and finding good ones too.

LESSON 7. Activities rather than stages. You probably won't experience stages of your imaginative process as a neat succession. For instance, after initially preparing yourself mentally, allowing ideas to incubate and having a first inspiration (which Wallas called Illumination), you are likely to find that you need to move back and forth between these activities as and when you need further ideas or to solve problems.

———

As Perkins pointed out in his critique of Wallas' proposal, stages are best thought of as activities within the imaginative process (6 pp. 183-5), and you may need to repeat them in different orders and several times during work on each project. Wallas, after all, was writing about how a single idea develops, not about the whole process of imaginative work. The lesson to take on board is not only that there are separate activities, but also that you should not expect to carry out these mechanically in a pre-set order.

LESSON 8. Learn the skills required for each activity. Once you have taken on board that imagining consists of more activities than just 'having an idea', recognise that there are distinct skills involved in each part of the process. Wallas gave advice which you could follow in order to improve your effectiveness in these separate activities. He explained that:

> At the Preparation stage we can consciously accumulate knowledge, divide up by logical rules the field of enquiry, and adopt a definite 'problem attitude'. In Verification we can consciously follow out rules like those used in Preparation. At the Incubation stage we can consciously arrange, either to think on other subjects than the proposed problem, or to rest from any form of conscious thought. (87 1945: viii)

He continued with other similar advice, and it seems to me significant that he repeatedly described 'consciously' intervening in the process. The point is that, once you've taken on board that 'imagining' consists of a series of separate activities, you can consciously intervene to help your imagination along at certain points. Of course, you should also make sure that you allow the necessary space and time for your subconscious to work away during other parts of the process.

Getting your head round the task - preparation

LESSON 9. Don't start by trying to find ideas, but first prepare. Think around all aspects of your project or problem, allow yourself time to reflect, and only after that start seeking ideas. As Mandler explained (76 p. 9), novel and creative acts require a prepared mind.

As an example, novelist Jeff VanderMeer described to an interviewer how, when planning to write about a specific character, '... before I go to bed, I will think consciously about the character and then wake up in the morning with some revelations.'(88 p. 18).

So, gather all the information on your problem or task, reflect on the task, then take a break and wait for ideas to appear. The ideas which come to you may not be like those you had expected or hoped to find, but there is nothing wrong with that. The process is subconscious, after all, and you should resist trying to control the outcome.

LESSON 10. Make both general and specific preparation. Webb Young, who I mentioned earlier, independently proposed the same set of stages of the imaginative process as Wallas, even though his book was published 13 years later. However, there were two key differences.

First, he explained that the raw material gathered in preparing should be both **specific** and **general** (7 p. 21), and that gathering general material should be a lifelong process (7 p. 26). Specific preparation, obviously, concerns your current project or problem. What he meant by general preparation was developing a knowledge and understanding of a wide range of subjects which may not seem immediately relevant to your imaginative project or field of work.

If you have this kind of wide-ranging knowledge, you might then notice parallels to your work in other fields, and these will aid you in your search for ideas helpful in your project. The implication is that you should avoid focusing narrowly on your own field, and instead learn to be curious about a wide range of subjects and events.

A series of practices based on the work of Leonardo were listed by Read, and these include the advice to 'Pursue interests and observations that may not have a clear purpose.' (4 p. 120). Doing this might seem a waste of time, but the point is that this will equip you with a variety of perspectives which may prove helpful in finding ideas or solving problems, as it presumably was to a person with such a remarkably wide-ranging imagination as Leonardo.

LESSON 11. Digest your material. The second point which Webb Young brought out more clearly than Wallas is that the background and information on your project or problem should not just be gathered, but that you should make sure you digest your material before seeking ideas.

This process of digesting your background material, or the different aspects of the problem you face, is partly a conscious activity, and it is distinct from the break from conscious thought during which ideas and solutions are most likely to appear.

As Webb Young put it, 'You take one fact, turn it this way and that, look at it in different lights, and feel for the meaning of it. You bring two facts together and see how they fit.' (7 p. 29). Here he was clearly describing a process of conscious analysis rather than subconscious rumination. The point is that preparation should not be seen just as a matter of listing the aspects of a task or problem, but analysing and digesting their every aspect. Only seek ideas after you have digested you task thoroughly.

LESSON 12. Spend time finding the problem. Following on from the previous lesson, the evidence is that spending time establishing what you are trying to make, or understanding the nature of the problem you are trying to solve, is crucial to the quality of your ideas. Parnes and his team reported on several studies which showed '... that the envisagement of the problem is central to the creative process ...' (74 p. 137). Jacob Getzels and Mihalyi Csikszentmihalyi also found, in a study of visual artists, that the '...time [they] spent on finding and formulating the problem ... correlates significantly with the evaluated worth of the drawings studied but the time spent working on it does not.' (89 p. 128).

You may be keen to crack on with your project, to start committing something to paper, or to spell out some ideas. Restrain yourself. Reflect further on your project or problem. The evidence is that better ideas will come if you spend more time reflecting on your what it is you are trying to achieve or solve, and if necessary redefining it.

LESSON 13. Be open to changing your view of your task. The more time you spend not only formulating, but also reformulating a problem, the better your ideas are likely to be. For instance, another finding of a study described by Getzels and Csikszentmihalyi was that the artists judged most creative were those who were more open to alternatives (89 p. 128).

Be prepared to spend time not only getting your head round what it is you are trying to do, but also on exploring various ways of looking at your project. You may find your thoughts go off in unexpected and valuable directions. Follow them, check out the options and alternatives, and don't rush to narrow your aims down prematurely.

LESSON 14. Know your subject and aim to be expert in your field. As Damasio put it, 'Great creators are highly expert, have extensive knowledge of their fields, and know what works and what doesn't.' (81 p. 64). He set out a series of requirements for creativity, which can be seen as skills you could acquire or attitudes you could learn and adopt:

- Motivation and courage
- Extensive experience and apprenticeship
- Insight into the workings of the self and into the workings of other minds
- Strong generation of representational diversity
- Large working memory
- Ability to recognise novel representations
- Sharply tuned decision-making apparatus (81 pp. 64-66).

It will be worth your while, not only spending plenty of time imagining, but also trying to develop skills of the type Damasio described. If you don't feel you know your subject well enough, work to improve your knowledge. Better and more useable ideas are more likely to come to people who understand their subject thoroughly.

LESSON 15. However, think like a beginner. There is a difficult balance to be struck between applying the expertise you have gained and yet remaining open to new possibilities as if you were a beginner. The risk for 'experts' is that their over-familiarity with approaches known to work well can lead them to being less open to new possibilities. Read therefore recommended '… adopting a beginner's mindset.' (4 p. 89), since this may free you from established approaches and your own habits, and, as he put it, 'help you to be open to the new and unexpected.' (4 p. 77).

He gave the example of the novelist Joseph Conrad, who was born in Poland, wrote his early novels in French, but changed to writing in English and then wrote the novels which are most widely-read nowadays. The change of language is likely to have enabled him to imagine anew without losing the novel-writing skills he had learned.

LESSON 16. Only connect. As E. M. Forster wrote in *Howards End*, 'Only connect the prose and the passion, and both will be exalted …' (90). He is thought to have been writing about the need to connect the means of expression with a deeper sense of feeling. On this subject, I referred earlier to Rossman's (72) finding that successful inventors engaged their feelings as they invented. Noordhof came to the same conclusion in his study, describing the imagination as an emotion-guided process (57 p. 337).

Take this on board, and allow yourself to become emotionally involved in your project from the start of your preparation. Learn to allow your feelings about the work grow and mature as you begin to imagine ideas. On the other hand, try to avoid becoming emotionally attached to specific ideas or approaches, since you may then fail to see their limitations.

LESSON 17. Explore alternatives before settling on your longer-term approach. Lu Liu's research team examined the development of 'hot streaks across artistic, cultural, and scientific' creative activity (91 p. 1), which they define as periods of intense productive activity. They gathered a wide range of data on many practitioners in each field.

They compared the extent and timing by the practitioners of, on the one hand, the exploration of a variety of subjects, approaches, or styles, and on the other a focus on the exploitation of just one of these. They found that '… hot streaks appear to be associated with neither exploration nor exploitation behavior in isolation, but a particular sequence of exploration followed by exploitation, where the transition from exploration to exploitation closely traces the onset of a hot streak.' (92 Abstract).

In other words, while constantly exploring different approaches may throw up many new ideas, the risk is that you may then not achieve as much as you might if you focused more narrowly. Equally, while exploiting one approach from the start is more likely to prove reliable in producing results, it may result in less originality. The implication of the research by Liu's team is that you would benefit from taking time, both early in each project and early in your work or life, to explore many approaches, styles, or types of idea or solution. You should then aim to exploit the approach or approaches which prove to be most productive.

Letting ideas develop – incubation

While ideas usually appear as if from nowhere with no conscious effort on your part, nevertheless there are skills you could learn which will help them mature in your subconscious. For example, Parnes and his team found that the most creative people were those who had learned to integrate unlike things, and to be open to making unexpected discoveries (74 p. 9).

In other words, they had learned ways of helping their subconscious minds to build the more distant connections which lead to the best ideas, and had also learned how to avoid preconceptions about their character obstruct the development of good ideas. There are several skills which you could learn or polish to help your subconscious process along in these and other ways.

LESSON 18. Let yourself default! Systems usually have a default mode of operation, and this is also true of your mental processes. When you relax your concentration or focus, the thoughts taking place within your Default Mode Network (DMN) come to the front of your mind. This network operates continuously, but when you stop focussing you become more conscious of the thoughts passing through it. The lessons in this section cover ways in which you could help your DMN to come to the fore, since this will allow ideas emerge more readily into your conscious mind.

Analyses by researchers of the DMN's operation show why allowing it to work more freely can help you find ideas. For instance, Kross described the DMN as transporting us to '... past events, imagined scenarios, and other internal musings.' (70 p. xx), and allowing us to 'run mental simulations [and to] explore different possible paths' (70 p. 13). A team led by Deniz Vatansever described the DMN similarly, as having an 'autopilot role' (111 p. 12821), and as making 'memory-based predictions to aid decision-making' (111 p. 12825).

This role in generating simulations and mental predictions (aka ideas) results from the DMN being 'the place where memories, which are a collection of events and knowledge about yourself, are housed. It's known to be the home of mind wandering, dreams, and daydreaming.' (40 p. 20), as Magsamen and Ross put it. They also describe how it acts as a filter helping consolidate memories most important to you.

As I noted in Chapter 1, the characteristics of the DMN are close to those of the concept of the subconscious dialogue. This dialogue is central to imagining since it leads to ideas forming. The DMN-derived thoughts which come to mind when you lose focus could be seen as these subconscious notions emerging into consciousness. They are often suppressed when you concentrate. This is why it is worth learning how to help your DMN operate more freely. Interesting new connections based on your memories are then more likely to emerge into consciousness as valuable ideas or alternatives.

LESSON 19. After preparing, don't try to find ideas. Take a break. After thinking around your project or problem, break and allow ideas to incubate. As an example, Mandler quoted Picasso explaining that, for the nature of his next painting to take shape in his mind, he needed to start with:

> '... contemplation, and I need long, idle hours of meditation. It is then that I work most. I look at

flies, at flowers, at leaves and trees around me. I let my mind drift at ease, just like a boat in the current. Sooner or later, it is caught by something. It gets precise. It takes shape – and my next painting motif is decided.' (74).

In the same vein, A. E. Housman is quoted as suggesting that the search for ideas will be helped if, after preparing, you then '... drink a pint of beer, relax, go walking, think on nothing in particular, look at things ...' (11 p. 475).

Follow the example of these highly creative people and take a break after preparing, since ideas and solutions to problems are more likely to occur to you when you are relaxed or thinking about other things.

LESSON 20. Stuck? Take a break. Breaks can be particularly valuable if the approach you are following isn't working out. Steven Smith described, for example, the risk of focusing on one possible solution and failing to explore alternatives (92 p. 147), and how this may lead to you feeling stuck. A break could solve a problem such as this.

As Mandler noted, if '... unsuccessful attempts at solutions are followed by a pause or delay ... [then] successful solutions are more probable.' (76 p. 16). Finke called this process '... helpful forgetting.' (93 p. 389) since it involves deliberately switching your focus away from the approach you were following, leaving you more open to finding fresh ideas.

Follow their advice, and take a break if you encounter problems. This will allow your imagination to wander more freely and maybe produce alternatives to ideas which are not working out, or help you identify weaknesses which can then be corrected. Give your subconscious the time and space to find alternatives and solutions to problems.

LESSON 21. Don't let yourself feel under pressure. Take a break instead. Rather than working harder in response to pressure, you are likely to find that ideas emerge more freely if you relax, let the pressure ebb away, and allow your mind to wander or drift into thinking about some other subject.

The Nobel Prize-winning writer Wole Soyinka gave the following excellent advice:

'I always advise the younger generation, don't submit to pressure. If you feel pressure of the sterile kind – which is, "I ought to write, I should write" – don't. Just go out and do something else. Immerse yourself in the environment. Go to a bar. Get drunk. Well, try not to get drunk but just do something else, something positive. ... You'll be astonished how quickly the material starts flowing in your mind.' (94 p. 57).

LESSON 22. Do something different. Breaking to do something other than your task can help you come up with ideas, and I quoted Wallas' advice on this earlier (87 p. viii). Mandler confirmed this in his research, finding that the incubation of ideas was more effective if '... the delay is filled with activities unrelated to the target material.' (76 p. 17).

Ap Dijksterhuis and Teun Meurs reported on a related study in which people were asked to come up with names for unfamiliar objects shown to them. The names suggested by people who came up with suggestions straight away were judged less original than those put forward by people who had been given another task to complete first (95 p. 87).

Try switching to another activity, and you may find this allows your subconscious mind to stray further and come up with more promising ideas.

LESSON 23. Do the washing up! One of Cameron's suggestions for breaking creative blocks was to do the washing up or a similar manual task which requires mental concentration (73 p. 196). Breaking from your work and focussing on the manual task – doing the filing, finally mending that doorbell, or doing exercise which requires mental concentration such as running – can help free your subconscious mind to work away and come up with ideas or solutions.

LESSON 24. Go for a walk. Walking doesn't require the same level of focus as the activities I mentioned in the previous lesson. However, it can be helpful because it allows for '... the mind's partial disengagement.' (4 p. 4), as Read explained. He also noted that it '... improves blood flow to the brain and [so] stimulates creative thinking.' (4 p. 285). As a result walking, especially walking outside where there is plenty to see and distract your conscious mind, allows your subconscious to work more freely.

Marily Oppezzo and Daniel Schwartz investigated this effect by asking different sets of people to come up with ideas when in various combinations of being seated and walking. They found that walking, especially walking outside, was the most productive approach (96 p. 1142). A review of research on this question, produced by May Wong for Stamford University, came to the same conclusion, with the output of ideas boosted by an average of 60% when walking (97). Wong mentioned that Steve Jobs was a noted walker, though apparently so is Mark Zuckerberg.

LESSON 25. 'To sleep, perchance to dream'.[2] Sleep and dreaming have been shown to help establish creative connections between distant experiences, and between feelings about experiences rather than their factual nature. Ullrich Wagner's research team found that sleep allows the intermingling of varied memories, and '… by restructuring new memory representations, [it] facilitates extraction of explicit knowledge and insightful behaviour.' (98 p. 352).

This takes place, as a team led by Robert Stickgold showed, because sleep and dreaming act as ways of consolidating '…associative memories…' (99 p. 1055), that is, the links and connections between your feelings about your memories rather than between their more 'factual' nature. They also noted that the brain is biased towards emotional rather than cognitive processing during the REM (rapid eye movement) sleep that is linked to dreaming.

This is exactly what you need in order to imagine effectively, so take on board the value of dozing, sleeping, and dreaming to help free your mind to explore more remote connections and generate valuable ideas.

---

[2] A metaphor Shakespeare gives Hamlet for his soliloquy debating suicide as a means of escape from the task of revenge imposed by his murdered father's ghost, which it has nothing to do with the beneficial effect of sleep in helping you find ideas!

LESSON 26. Explore the sweet spot before sleep. There is a short period when we feel we are about to fall asleep but are not fully unconscious. Ideas are particularly likely to appear when we are in this state.

Célia Lacaux's research team studied this '... creative sweet spot within the sleep-onset period' and noted that 'hitting it requires individuals balancing falling asleep easily against falling asleep too deeply.' (100). They explained that, since creative work depends on the interplay of the conscious and subconscious mind, the moment of drifting off can be particularly productive of ideas. After all, we not only need to have ideas, but to become aware of them.

In their experiment, they presented the participants with a problem and then gave them a '... 20-min break (Break phase) during which they were asked to relax in a semi-reclined position with their eyes closed.' (100). This proved productive in generating solutions to the problem.

They quoted the example of inventor Thomas Edison, who reportedly napped while holding spheres in his hands. He reckoned that the spheres would drop noisily as soon as he fell fully asleep, waking him up just in time to capture any ideas which had come to him as he dropped off. They tested this approach and found that it was productive. So, invest in some spheres, settle down for a nap, and wait for your light-bulb moment.

LESSON 27. Don't let your conscious mind interfere. Vaune Ainsworth-Land advised the 'abandonment of conscious striving' (101 p. 24) as a way of helping ideas emerge. On this theme, George Sakkal carried out a study of the importance of gut feeling and subconscious thought in creative work, and recommended trying to avoid your conscious mind spoiling the ideas which emerge (102). He quoted the research which I referred to in the previous chapter which showed that subconscious processes can lead to both the ideas forming and decisions being taken before we become fully aware of that either has happened.

He went on to caution against allowing the conscious mind to take over the imaginative process prematurely since the results could be less valuable than they might otherwise have been. He quoted the painter Paul Cézanne, who said that 'If the artist ... dares to interfere deliberately with what he has to convey, then his own mediocrity filters through. The work produced is inferior.'(102 p. 153).

The point is that the subconscious mind has greater ability than the conscious mind to form the unexpected connections from which more original ideas develop. You may later decide not to use the ideas, but that is a separate issue which I'll deal with later.

LESSON 28. Allow mental disorder to reign. Mental chaos can be helpful when you are trying to come up with ideas. As Finke explained, '... chaotic thinkers are often better at seeing remote associations and connections, particularly those that cut across traditional conceptual boundaries.' (93 p. 390).

The poet Paul Valéry is quoted as saying that '... disorder is the condition of the mind's fertility.' (37 p. 317). Ideas which arrive through chaotic thinking may have greater potential because they result from your subconscious mind building connections between previously unrelated memories of a kind you would have been less likely to make through more orderly conscious or concentrated thought.

Learn to allow your mind to flit from one thing to another, since new and more distant links may then be formed more readily, leading to promising ideas emerging from your subconscious. These are less likely to form through concentrated and conscious thought.

LESSON 29. Relax, hesitate, allow doubts. John Dewey in his classic study, *How We Think*, noted that reflective thinking involves:

> (1) a state of doubt, hesitation, perplexity, mental difficulty, in which thinking originates, and (2) an act of searching, hunting, inquiring, to find material that will resolve the doubt, settle and dispose of the perplexity. (103 p. 12)

In the same vein, Koestler suggested 'thinking aside' (37 p. 163) when you feel stuck. He meant allowing your mind to wander onto other matters (see next lesson) to permit the formation of new connections. These may help free your imagination when it has become blocked. Valuable ideas will emerge when they are good and ready.

Hesitation may also help, as Parnes and his team suggested, since additional subconscious reflection may result in ideas appearing which had not previously occurred to you (74 p. 9). Better ideas or ways of solving problems could well come to mind if you delay deciding about the initial thoughts which come to you.

LESSON 30. Allow your mind to wander. Closely connected to the previous point is the evidence that mind-wandering appears to be more effective than concentrated thought in generating creative ideas. Davies, for instance, quoted research pointing to the value of mind wandering in generating ideas (35 p. 162).

Mind wandering may also be more effective in creative work than mindfulness training. In their research, Claire Zedelius and Jonathan Schooler (104) asked people to find solutions through mindful and analytic approaches or by allowing their minds to wander.

The 'mindful' participants in their study had been trained to develop a greater awareness of the operation of their minds in the present moment. They were more effective in finding solutions, but these were judged to be less creative than those produced by the participants who allowed their minds to wander.

However, a recent summary of research on this subject by Dannah Henriksen and her team came to the conclusion that '... mindfulness can support creativity.' (105), though they also noted that the connection between the two is not simple. The jury is still out on mindfulness maybe.

It does seem clear from this research, however, that letting your mind wander can help you come up with good ideas, though only if you have first prepared thoroughly of course.

LESSON 31. Allow yourself to be bored. Boredom need not be experienced as wholly negative, as Sandi Mann and Rebekah Cadman found in their study since, as they explain, it '...can have positive outcomes, one of which might be increased creativity.' (106 p. 165)

Benjamin Baird's team also found that giving people an undemanding task was more effective in helping them come up with solutions than giving a demanding task, allowing rest, or allowing no break (107 p. 1117). The undemanding task led to boredom and mind-wandering, and these helped ideas arrive more readily. Boredom has this effect because it leads to a search for more variety and so to increased activity in the subconscious mind.

For example, while we can't now know whether Einstein was bored in his routine job at the Swiss Patent Office, but his mind clearly wasn't fully occupied by his work tasks since it was during this time that he began to develop the theory of relativity, widely seen as be the most important scientific break-through of the Twentieth Century.

So, if you are stuck, allow yourself to be bored. Since your conscious mind will then be less engaged, your sense of boredom, which after all amounts to a lack of conscious mental engagement, can allow your subconscious to work more freely, leading to the appearance of ideas.

LESSON 32. Think divergently. A good way of helping your subconscious to explore ideas and alternatives is to range over many possibilities rather than settling on one prematurely. This is the essence of divergent thinking. Allowing yourself to flit between many possibilities until you settle (converge) on one has been found to be a good way of producing promising ideas.

Both Michele Kaschub (108) and the team of Dijksterhuis and Meurs (95 p. 137) explained that divergent thinking, as opposed to convergent thinking, in which you bring ideas together to focus on the task in hand, is less conscious and so more likely to lead to creative answers.

Peter Webster went on from this to describe the alternation between divergent and convergent thinking as the essence of creativity (109 p. 26), since divergent thinking is helpful in coming up with ideas, but convergent thinking is important in choosing ideas or deciding on possible applications.

This suggests that your search for ideas will be more likely to meet with success if you allow your thoughts to diverge from your starting point and range over many possibilities in the early stages. In particular, avoid settling on the first idea you come up with, even if it seems excellent to you. Instead, allow yourself to wonder about alternatives, and only then make choices.

Helping ideas appear – illumination

As I described in the previous chapter, you don't so much <u>have</u> ideas as find yourself 'in possession' of them, as composer Aaron Copland put it (110 p. 42). They just appear in your mind. Even so, there are skills you can learn which could help ideas come to you in this apparently passive way.

As you will probably see as I continue, there is a fine line between the approaches described in the previous section which may help your subconscious dialogue to work more freely, and the suggestions set out here for helping ideas to finally appear in your conscious mind. This is not surprising since the first of these two activities within the imaginative process leads directly to the second.

LESSON 33. Relax! Have a drink! The evidence is that relaxing can help free the creative juices. Drinking alcohol tends to make you relaxed, and has been shown to improve your chances of finding ideas.

For instance, research by Andrew Jorosz and his team found that moderate intoxication gave people an advantage in standard creative problem-solving tasks (112 p. 1142). This advantage appears to have resulted from the alcohol helping relaxation, which then allowed ideas to appear more readily in their conscious minds. Concentrating too hard can block the creative juices, while relaxation, whether helped by alcohol or not, can allow ideas to emerge more freely.

However, disabuse yourself of the idea that drug taking can assist creativity, an idea reflected in the stereotype of the drug-taking writer or musician. A summary of research by Jennifer Haase's team concluded that, of all the factors associated with enhanced creativity, 'Complex training courses, meditation and cultural exposure were most effective … while the use of cognitive manipulation drugs was least and also non-effective.' (113).

Stay off the drugs and follow the advice in this book instead.

LESSON 34. Accept what arrives. Having a preconceived view of the type of ideas for which you are looking can block their emergence, as Finke described, and he recommended allowing new forms of combination between elements to come to you freely (93 p. 383). The result may be that the ideas you find are unlike those you had hoped for.

They can even appear so strange to you that it may seem as if they had come from another person. Artists, for instance, have described a person separate from themselves who is the source of their ideas, and whom they call 'the artist' (114 p. 50). As novelist Nick Harkaway put it, 'Writing is always some kind of encounter with another person that lives in your head ...' (115 p. 11). The same will be true of any other imaginative activity once you learn to allow your subconscious to work freely.

While the process by which ideas are formed may take place within your subconscious mind, the ideas of course arise from memories formed through wide ranging social and environmental interactions and influences. As a result, they are never just 'your ideas', so it should not surprise you if the ideas which appear in your mind may at times seem strange or even foreign.

Another reason you may be surprised by your ideas, as a team led by Kenneth Bowers found, is that '... people are able to respond productively to information that they do not consciously notice or remember ...' (116 p. 29). As a result, there may be information or experiences which you have absorbed subconsciously and which nevertheless feed into your ideas.

Since you do not have conscious control over your imaginative process, you should learn to just accept the ideas which arrive. (But see the section on Evaluation below.)

LESSON 35. Free your mind to play. Finke mentioned studies by Getzels and Czikszentmihalyi (89) and Perkins (6) in which they found that '... combinatorial play ...', or messing around with possible ideas, was valuable in creative work (93 p. 383). He also described a study in which people came up with more creative suggestions about the nature of an object if they didn't know the category into which it fell (93 pp. 383-5), since this left them freer to play around with possible definitions.

The lesson of their research is to allow yourself to play around with many possibilities and alternatives. You may eventually come up with different, and perhaps more valuable, ideas than those you has expected to find, and they may be quite unlike those you had been expecting to find.

LESSON 36. BUT, limit the scope of your search. There is nothing worse than a blank sheet of paper, except perhaps constraints which straitjacket your search for ideas. Limits, but limits which are not too tight, were shown to stimulate the imagination in studies by both Catrinel Haught-Tromp (117) and Jim Bright and Robert Pryor's team (118).

Haught-Tromp concluded that '… creativity depends on constraints, which limit the overwhelming number of available choices.' Some freedom from constraints is needed in order to imagine, but too much freedom can leave you with an empty mind, since it is then hard to know where to start. If you want ideas to emerge freely from your subconscious mind, you should try setting limits to the scope of your search for ideas – limits which are not too tight, but limits nevertheless.

LESSON 37. Delay final choices, remain open to changes. Perkins recommended remaining open to many possibilities in the early stages of work, and only narrowing down later, remaining willing to revise earlier decisions, and avoiding settling on the first ideas which arrive (6 p. 187). He quoted a study of artists which found that 'the artists rated best were not those who imagined they had produced fixed and finished works, but those who recognized the possibility of change.' (6 p. 159).

Take your time, delay your choices, and accept that changes remain possible up to the point where you really feel your project is complete (See section on Completing below).

LESSON 38. Make mistakes, notice chance occurrences. You may make 'mistakes', or accidentally record an idea differently from how you thought you had imagined it. Stop yourself from correcting these straight away since, if you reflect a little, you might come to see them as improvements or alternatives. Perkins discussed the potential value of accidents and mistakes, and suggested that you may find they turn out to be interesting alternatives or possibilities.

He quoted Louis Pasteur, the French scientist who made discoveries key to the development of vaccines, and who famously said that 'Chance favours the prepared mind.' (6 p. quoted 283). Perkins' view was that being aware and noticing things which occur by chance, or spotting errors or flaws and deciding to make use of them, is a vital skill in imaginative work as long as, like Pasteur, you have first prepared by spending time getting your head round your task.

Another reason for not rejecting your 'mistakes' out of hand is that they might, of course, result from a subconscious reaction to the nature of your task or problem.

LESSON 39. Think counter-factually. Adam Galinsky led a research team which found that '... one could increase peoples' chance of finding a solution by getting them into a "counterfactual mindset" that encouraged mental stimulation.' (119 p. 384). Another team he led found that 'counterfactuals prime a mental simulation mind-set that leads people to consider alternatives.' (120 p. 252).

The implication of these teams' findings is that developing the habit of thinking about how things might be different could lead you to find better ideas or solutions. For instance, try reflecting on:

- whether maybe you should be asking yourself a different question.
- whether there might be another and better way of viewing your task.
- whether you've overlooked aspects of a problem.
- what else might be at the root of a difficulty you are finding.
- whether starting at a different place in the project might prove productive.
- whether doing the opposite to your current plan might lead to a better solution.

Thought processes such as these could help you to come up with more promising ideas, or might lead you to developing your project in new and positive directions which would not otherwise have occurred to you.

LESSON 40. Value the complexity embedded in ideas. As Kounios and Beeman found, when solutions arrive through sudden insight after subconscious thought, this follows increased activity in part of the brain which makes connections between distantly related information (32 p. 70). Ideas which arrive suddenly will have been formed through a process of subconscious rumination through which links, often unexpected, will have been made between different memories.

Ideas which arrive in this way can have many potential meanings and connotations, and so they are likely to come across in contrasting ways to different people. This is not a problem, since more people will be able to engage with your ideas if each of them is able to perceive the ideas in their own unique way.

This is why it can be productive to train yourself to stand aside mentally and allow your subconscious to make the new and complex re-combinations between memories and experiences which lie behind the best and most innovative ideas. Resist simplifying ideas which arrive, at least until you have evaluated them thoroughly in the ways I'll describe later.

LESSON 41. Be aware, listen. You may be able to sense that an idea is about to come to you before it actually arrives. As I explained in the previous chapter, neurologists Kounios and Beeman (32) and Konečni (30) noted activity in key areas of the brain <u>before</u> a person became conscious of an idea. It is possible to sense this process of an idea is forming in your subconscious.

Wallas called this Intimation, and recommended trying to become aware that an idea is forming and protecting this process from interruption (87 p. viii). Follow his advice. If you sense an idea forming, don't rush to pin it down. The idea will appear in its own good time.

LESSON 42. An idea arrives. 'Insights occur when subconsciously activated ideas pop into awareness ...', as Kounios and Beeman put it (32 p. 86), and these moments of insight may follow an extended process. This is reflected by the fact that I've only arrived at this point after covering a great deal of other ground.

There are other mental activities which precede the arrival of an idea, and so it was important to describe them first. Learning the skills required for those other activities will help improve the number and quality of the ideas which develop and eventually pop into your mind.

Think of yourself as a vessel in which a brew (an idea) matures, perhaps slowly, rather than as an active maker of ideas, so learn and practise the skills required in this brewing process.

Imagine for your public, imagine in your medium

LESSON 43. Think of your public before starting work. While coming up with ideas which please you is important, there is a risk that these ideas may not work for your public – and there is almost always some form of public for ideas. It is important to remember that each member of your public will, potentially, see your ideas differently from the way you do. To help ensure your ideas come across effectively, it is important to think of your public during your preparation, and then to imagine with them in mind.

If you feel you don't know enough about how your public will receive ideas, find out more about them and then ditch ideas which you then decide are unlikely to come across effectively. 'Market research' of this kind is important in all imaginative work, and it is a good way of helping filter out ideas unlikely to work for your public.

LESSON 44. Connect with existing perceptions and app-roaches. Your public are more likely to be able to relate to your ideas if they can see connections to things with which they are familiar. Helping them to make connections of this type will give you a basis for then moving on to new ground without leaving your audience behind. In any case, trans-formational ideas which have no connection with the existing state of the your field, or with the traditions and app-roaches used previously, do not really exist.

As I explained in the previous chapter, all imaginative work takes place in the context of previous ideas in the same or other fields, even if it takes the form of a rebellion against established practice. Ideas grow out of your memories, and these result from your experiences of the world as it already exists, which includes current and past traditions and practices.

To give an example, in the early decades of the Twentieth Century composer Arnold Schoenberg developed a way of writing music using all twelve notes in the Western scale in a repeated sequence, and in this way he broke free from the system of musical keys (C major etc.) which had dominated for centuries. However, his new method of composing was in fact a natural development of the style he and others had been developing in the years before its invention.

Schoenberg explained that he saw himself as working forward from existing traditions and not as a revolutionary seeking their overthrow (121 p. 137). All new ideas draw and build on existing ideas, styles, and approaches in this way. I don't believe in the existence of ideas which are wholly unconnected with previous ideas.

LESSON 45. Let ideas come to you in your medium. If you develop adverts, imagine adverts. If you design buildings, imagine buildings, and so on. As composer Kaija Saariaho wrote, 'The material can come from our own lives, the lives around us, or wherever. But at some point, it simply becomes music.' (122). This is how the artists I quoted at the start of Chapter 1 imagined. The composer imagined in music, the playwright in dialogue, and so on.

That is how ideas develop, in the medium of expression you are using, without explanation, but out of the interactions between your accumulated memories. This apparently passive process will work most effectively if you avoid starting your search for ideas by defining or describing what you are trying to communicate.

Specifying what you are looking for at the start of your project can risk constraining your imagination and blocking the emergence of good ideas. Instead, once you have all aspects of the problem in your mind, let ideas come to you in the medium in which you work. The ideas which arrive may surprise you and lead to positive solutions, or take you in interesting directions.

LESSON 46. Avoid verbal explanations. Imagining in your own medium will be most effective if you avoid imposing a verbal explanation on your ideas prematurely.

I mentioned the view of ancient Sanskrit scholars that there is a pre-verbal stage to imagining (87 p. 53). Modern research by Jonathan Schooler and Joseph Melcher supports the idea that you should avoid interrupting the sense of an idea developing by verbalising it. They studied the difficulty of verbalising or explaining emerging ideas and concluded that '... verbalization can interfere with ... non-reportable processes.' (123 p. 108), that is, the process of ideas forming.

Describing your ideas in words can result in you finding yourself stuck with ones that are only half formed because you tried to pin them down before they were good and ready.

Also, don't try to judge your ideas by explaining them. Words can certainly never adequately convey the sense of non-verbal ideas. Even ideas which consist of words are usually their own best explanation. If you find that a further verbal explanation of verbally-expressed ideas helps it is probable that there is something lacking in the original.

In any case, verbal explanations you offer will reflect just your own perception of your ideas, and other people may legitimately see the ideas differently.

LESSON 47. The reason - thinking is not, initially, verbal. Research on this subject, summarised in two articles by Michael Gazzaniga (124) (125)[3] shows that the holistic thinking which leads to the appearance of ideas depends more on the operation of the right hemisphere of the brain, which is less involved in verbalisation in the right-handed 90% of

---

[3] Among the many studies he summarised were those by Thomas Bever and Robert Chiarello (133), George Wolford's team (142), and Martin Lotze's team (136).

people, whereas analytic and verbal thought depends more on the left.

Iain McGilchrist went on from this to show that ideas are conceived holistically first, and that we only try to explain them in words after they have started to take shape (126 p. 72). The Roman poet, Horace, expressed this as follows:

> For nature has so formed us that we feel inwardly any changes in our fortunes … it is only afterwards that she expresses these feelings in us by means of the tongue. (127 p. 101)

Avoid interrupting your holistic imagination by explaining your ideas in words. Instead, let yourself feel them 'inwardly'. If possible in your field, allow your ideas to explain themselves without further verbal commentary, and always avoid narrowing ideas down by offering verbal summaries or explanations prematurely.

Before pressing on – evaluate your ideas

Evaluating ideas before making use of them is essential to the success in any kind of imaginative work. Wallas called this 'verification' (87 p. viii), and may well have used that term since he was analysing descriptions of the experiences of the imaginative process by scientists and mathematicians. I prefer to call this evaluation since that term applies more widely.

LESSON 48. Don't fall in love – with your ideas. So, you have some ideas. You feel pleased with them. Stop! Learn to look at your ideas critically before pressing on. As Webb Young put it, 'In this stage you have to take your little newborn idea out into the world of reality. And when you do you usually find it is not quite the marvellous child it seemed when you first gave birth to it.' (7 p. 38).

Learn to allow time to evaluate ideas to find their faults, then eliminate these and evaluate your ideas again. Don't assume that coming up with ideas is the end of the process.

LESSON 49. Take on board what evaluation really means. Evaluation involves looking at your ideas critically, and asking whether you feel sure they are just right. Learn to stand back from your ideas to view them in a detached way.

You should think about how the ideas would seem to other people, whether they might be improved if they were a little different, or even substantially revised. Perhaps one 'idea' is actually a bundle of ideas which needs to be split apart. Perhaps another idea might work better if it were turned around another way or upside-down ... and I could go on.

The key is to keep an open mind about your initial ideas, examine them with a critical eye, and then re-work and revise them as necessary until you feel sure they are right. You will know you have completed your evaluation when the sense comes to you that your ideas are just right.

LESSON 50. Don't (necessarily) use all your ideas. You may have a whole set of ideas for a project, but the first step could be to reject many of them or maybe put them aside for other projects. Remember that your public will come across your ideas afresh, and won't be familiar with them in the way you are.

You need to help your public 'get it first time', to some extent at least, otherwise they may find it hard to engage with your ideas. If you present them with too many ideas at once, or a complex idea which they struggle to get their heads round, you will have failed.

Learn to ditch ideas if you have too many for your project, or to simplify them if they are too complex. Maybe split complex ideas up into their component parts and use these parts separately.

LESSON 51. Don't flog dead horses. Sometimes you should just accept that your idea might simply be weak or wrong. The American music teacher Bruce Adolfe explained that you may '... feel that it's [an idea's] not what you wanted; it's not what you set out to say ... it may be very good, but you no longer find it ... an expression of what you had in mind.' (129 p. 72).

In a famous example, Franz Schubert's 'Unfinished' Symphony consists of two complete movements and an incomplete third, whilst the usual concluding fourth is missing. It is widely accepted that a piece Schubert wrote to accompany a play is actually the missing last movement. Beardsley suggests that Schubert gave up the struggle to complete the third movement, and so the symphony, because the musical idea he came up with was dull but compulsive (128 p. 300). As a result, he couldn't see how to continue.

I played in a performance of a version of the Symphony completed by a modern composer, and I can testify that the third movement idea is dull. Accept, like Schubert, that if your idea feels wrong to you then it _is_ wrong, or wrong for the project concerned.

You are bound to realise as you evaluate your ideas that some are really simply not going to work out, so put them aside and search for alternatives.

LESSON 52. If your idea feels wrong, try to work out why. The sense that an idea feels right or wrong comes from your subconscious, but there will be reasons for this sense and you may be able to work out what they are. As Perkins explained, 'Critical response is predominantly non-analytical but also nonintuitive – free of overt reasoning and intentional analysis but full of reasons.' (6 p. 109).

If you feel dissatisfied with an idea, you can often work out the reasons why you feel this way, and this could help you revise it to solve the problem. Perkins suggested trying to spot difficulties by standing back from your idea and then looking to see what is wrong (6 p. 113), or trying to spot problems which might arise in using it. If an idea doesn't feel right, analyse it in these and other ways to identify what is causing your sense of dissatisfaction.

LESSON 53. Find the problem; reformulate; repeat. Parnes and his team recommended that you should see yourself as a '... problem finder as well as a problem solver.' (74 p. 9). They meant that you should always try to pick holes in your idea or plan before going on, rather than deciding to make use of it uncritically.

You should then reformulate your idea if necessary and be willing to rework each idea repeatedly until you are really satisfied with the result.

LESSON 54. Try it differently (Part 1). Once you have an idea, spend time playing around with it, and try alternative forms of the idea or different ways of using it. This may lead to a version that is closer to your sense of what you want, or the discovery of ways of using the idea that hadn't previously occurred to you.

For example, Brewster Ghiselin described Beethoven's sketching and re-sketching a theme for one of his piano sonatas, explaining that '... the sketches show him carefully modelling, then testing in systematic and apparently cold-blooded fashion, the theme of the fugue. Where, one might ask, is the inspiration here?' (64 p. 47). The answer, Ghiselin argued, is that Beethoven had an initial idea, but then needed to work through different versions until he found the one which he felt was exactly right.

Learn to do the same, and work out alternative versions or applications of an idea before going further.

LESSON 55. Try it differently (Part 2). Try adding or taking away parts of your idea, approaches which Davies called additive and subtractive imagination. Additive thinking obviously involves adding elements to your idea. Davies explained that it '... encourages a more expansive mindset, which helps with creativity' (35 p. 189) and may result in improvements to your initial idea.

Subtractive thinking involves looking at how an idea might seem if elements were taken away. A simplified idea might come across more clearly and effectively than the original. There are, obviously, risks involved in narrowing down in this way so that an idea becomes oversimplified, just as there are risks in adding too much to an idea so it becomes too complex to be readily understood by your public.

However, it can be worth spending time taking away elements from your idea or adding them to see whether these changes lead to improvements. Do this before you go on to make more extensive use of your idea.

LESSON 56. Ask yourself, where does it lead? A lesson I learned from an eminent composer, and one of my teachers, was stop and ask myself some questions once I had found an idea which felt right. To ask, for instance: what are its implications; where does it lead; how can I develop it into something larger?

This interrogation is an important part of the process of ensuring that an idea or plan will work well. Skipping this stage of evaluation can mean that you find later that your idea leads nowhere or doesn't work well when used in a more extended way.

Spend time thinking about where your idea is going and how it could be used before you go any further. You may decide to revise or reject your initial idea if the direction in which it leads seems unlikely to contribute to your project, even if you like the idea. It is best to do this early on to avoid wasting time on an idea which turns out not to contribute positively to your current project.

LESSON 57. Seek feedback. The most valuable thing you can receive is feedback, so never hesitate to ask colleagues or teachers for help. Their role should not be to tell you what to do, but to help you learn to be self-critical.

Webb Young suggested asking for reactions to ideas, and recommended that you should submit any developing idea '… to the criticism of the judicious' (7 p. 39). Perkins also found in his survey of studies that feedback helps in producing better work. For instance, he quoted a study of poets rated according to the quality of their verse which showed that '… the better-rated poets sought and valued criticism significantly more.' (6 p. 124).

Feedback can also help you learn to be self-critical. Getzels and Csikszentmihalyi reported on a study in which that a panel who rated artists' work '… found that the artists rated best were not those who imagined they had produced fixed and finished works, but those who recognized the possibility of change.' (89 p. 159). They had learned to be self-critical, and the result was that their work was rated more highly.

Never underestimate the value of feedback. As and when you receive it, use it to teach yourself how to be your own, self-critical, teacher.

LESSON 58. Evaluate more, imagine better. The more time you spend evaluating your ideas, the better you will become at generating ideas to start with. This is because the habits you develop in evaluation will become incorporated into your imaginative process. Ideas with less potential will then be quickly filtered out or barely reach the level of your conscious mind.

As Perkins put it, drawing on a wealth of research findings, 'The properties the maker imparts to the product in after-the-fact, corrective ways gradually become imparted in original acts of production.' (6 p. 129).

If you learn and apply the skills required for evaluating ideas, these will become habits of thought which will help you come up with better ideas to start with.

Completing and finishing

At some point you will decide that you have evaluated your ideas sufficiently thoroughly, and they are now ready for use in your project. Later you will need to decide if the project is complete. Again, there are skills which can be learned and used in this decision-making.

LESSON 59. Wait till your ideas are properly cooked. The sense that an idea is right and ready for use, or that a project is complete, does not come simply from conscious, logical, analysis but involves the subconscious. You need to learn to wait until this subconscious sense of rightness or completeness develops.

For instance, Yul Kang's team found that '... awareness of having reached a decision appears to arise when the brain's representation of accumulated evidence reaches a threshold or bound.' (130 p. 1), and they based this on a study of people who were asked to report the moment when they '... felt they had decided in their mind.' (130 p. 9).

This threshold is reached when you subconsciously sense there is nothing further wrong or unsatisfactory. Your subconscious is better than your conscious mind at weighing up the many aspects and implications of an idea in order to decide whether it is right and ready for use, or somehow 'wrong'.

Avoid deciding to make use of an idea, or declaring a project finished, if you sense any remaining niggles of doubt. Wait until you feel sure.

LESSON 60. Allow time for review. Perkins recommended setting a project aside when it seems to be complete, but then coming back to it after a time (6 p. 286). If you have a deadline, aim to complete your project in advance, take a break, and then have a final look. Develop this habit of setting yourself an advance deadline so you have time to come back to your work. You may then notice problems you had previously been unable to see.

LESSON 61. Step back for a better view. One problem which can arise when you are immersed in developing your idea or project is that you may fail to see its overall shape or implications clearly. Before you decide your project is finished, learn to stand back and view it as a whole, while also trying to look at it from the point of view of your public.

Perkins described a skill he calls 'hill climbing' (6 p. 285), by which he meant the ability to step some distance away from your work to see at it as a whole as if you were viewing a town from a hill. You may then notice flaws or problems which you couldn't see before because you were too close to your work.

LESSON 62. Accept that ideas have a life of their own. Your idea or project may not have developed in the way you expected, or along the lines of a plan you made at the start because your subconscious imagination may have led you in directions you had not anticipated. This should not necessarily trouble you, and you should avoid rejecting the results of your imaginative work without good reason.

As Ghiselin explained, for musical composition, the process of working involves:

> ... first of all ... of listening inwardly to the music
> as it shapes itself; of allowing the music to grow;
> of following both inspiration and conception
> wherever they may lead. (64 p. 48)

You will be able to think of parallels in your own activities or work. Ideas have their own dynamic, and it is a mistake to try to control where they lead. Allow them to develop in their own way, but compare any new directions they take with your original thoughts, and think constantly about whether your plan might need to change in the light of the way your ideas are evolving.

Obviously, your ideas might have led you away from the key aims of the project. If so, ask yourself why, since maybe the aims need revising. If you decide the aims are correct, park the ideas, maybe use them in another project, and start again.

LESSON 63. Have a plan, but don't be rigid. You may have made a plan for your project at the start of your work. It is as much an act of the imagination to develop a plan for the overall shape of a project as it is to come up with individual ideas, and all the advice given so far applies equally to planning.

You may of course find a plan takes shape slowly as you begin to work out the implications of your initial ideas, or that your thoughts about the plan change as you work on the project. This is why you should avoid sticking rigidly to a plan made at the start. Equally, pressing on with no sense of plan or direction can result in incoherence.

One of the many composers interviewed by Ann McCutchan described having an initial concept, often working out a detailed plan, but then changing the plan in implementation if the developing ideas turn out to lead in a different direction (131 p. 77). This is a good approach.

LESSON 64. Remember how planning works. Planning in imaginative work should never mean deciding your whole structure and end point when you start work on a project. You may have a fairly detailed view on how your project should begin, but it is often worth leaving later parts less defined, even if you have a general notion of where you are going. Allow the ideas you come up with to lead you towards the most appropriate conclusion.

Perkins made a series of suggestions on planning a project, some of which point in different directions. That doesn't mean that they are contradictory, only that there are competing pressures to be reconciled in planning. He listed four approaches:

---

1. Planning – making a plan for the work rather than producing it directly.
2. Abstracting – taking ideas from wherever rather than working from general intentions to particulars.
3. Undoing – being willing to undo and redo.
4. Making means [the way you go about something] into ends, that is, allowing the way you work to have an effect on the final form of your project (6 p. 276).

Try to bear all these things in mind, and avoid a rigid approach or a plan set in concrete at the start.

LESSON 65. Learn to recognise that, when it feels finished, it is finished. I've mentioned several times the subconscious sense that an idea 'feels' right or wrong. This also applies to a project. The feeling of rightness results from the development in your subconscious mind of a sense of satisfaction with the whole project. A conscious or verbal assessment of an idea will always, by contrast, be narrower.

There is, of course, a risk of failing to assess your own sense of rightness or completeness in an entirely honest way. You may find that preferences or attitudes not really relevant to the development of your idea or project distract you from allowing your true sense of 'rightness' to come through.

One reason why you could fall into this trap might be that you feel proud of your ideas, or fond of them, whereas you should be ruthless in evaluating them. Learn to guard against these risks.

Judge your idea or project in terms of how you honestly feel about it, and make this judgement by standing back and reviewing it in as detached way as possible. In particular, try to see it as if you were one of your own audience.

If you still have a niggling feeling that something is not quite right, evaluate the idea or project again, and try to identify and eliminate the source of the niggle.

A sense that your project really is complete may then come to you, since you will finally feel that there are no unresolved problems or issues. Then you will know that it is finished.

Conclusion

You probably already know and use some of the approaches suggested here. Others are likely to be new to you. In any case, I think I've suggested enough ways in which you could improve your skills to show that a good imagination is not a gift, but depends on a set of skills that anyone could apply to help them imagine more effectively.

Specifically, I hope I've shown that it is worth preparing thoroughly by analysing and thinking around your project, taking a breather to allow your subconscious the time to generate ideas, and waiting patiently till ideas appear. It is then worth evaluating your ideas and their potential implications and applications rigorously, and revising them as necessary.

After that you will benefit from allowing your imagination to play with possible ways of applying the ideas or solutions on which you settle and, finally, reflecting about whether you are really satisfied with the way your complete project has turned out.

Of course, it is important not to apply the lessons set out here in a mechanical way. Your aim should instead be to integrate those approaches you find helpful into your way of working. They will then gradually become habits of thought, and will no longer be lessons you need to learn.

References

1. **Vygotsky, Lev.** *Mind in Society: The Development of Higher Psychological Processes.* Cambridge : Harvard Unversity Press, 1978.

2. **Piaget, Jean.** *The Child's Conception of the World.* New York : International Universities Press, 1929.

3. **Hirsh-Pasek, Kathy & Roberta Michnick Golinkoff.** *Einstein Never Used Flashcards: How children really learn and why they need to play more and memorise less.* Emmaus PA : Rodale Books, 2003.

4. **Read, Albert.** *The Imagination Muscle: Where good ideas come from (and how to have more of them).* London : Little, Brown Book Group , 2023.

5. **Sawyer, Keith, Vera John-Steiner, Seana Moran, Robert J. Sternberg, David Henry Feldman, Jenne Nakamura, Mihalyi Csikszentmihalyi.** *Creativity and Development.* Oxford & New York : Oxford University Press, 2003.

6. **Perkins, D.N.** *The Mind's Best Work.* Cambridge MA : Harvard University Press, 1981.

7. **Webb Young, James.** *A Technique for Producing Ideas.* New York & London : McGraw-Hill, 2003.

8. **Taylor, Alan.** *The Imagination of Experiences: Musical invention, collaboration, and the making of meanings.* Abingdon : Routledge, 2021.

9. **Hamburger, Michael.** *Beethoven: Letters, Journals and Conversation.* New York : Thames & Hudson, 1992.

10. **Sillitoe, Alan.** *The Loneliness of the Long Distance Runner.* London & New York : Harper Perennial, 2007.

11. **Wimsatt, William K. & Monroe C. Beardsley.** The Intentional Fallacy. Book auth. William K. Wimsatt. *The Verbal Icon: Studies in the Meaning of Poetry.* Lexington : University of Kentucky Press, 1954, pp. 3-20.

12. **Taverner, John.** *The Music of Silence: A Composer's Testament.* London : Faber & Faber, 1999.

13. **Pinter, Harold.** Nobel Lecture: Art, Truth & Politics. *Nobelprize.org, Nobel Media AB.* 2005. http://www.nobelprize.org/nobel_prizes/literature/laureates/2005/pinter-lecture-e.html. [Viewed: 2 1 2017.]

14. **Plato.** *Apology.* Cabin John, MY : Wildside Press, 2016.

15. **Bible, The.** *Authorized Version.* London : The British and Foreign Bible Society, 1957.

16. **Solms, Mark.** *The Hidden Spring: A Journey to the Source of Consciousness.* London : Profile Books, 2021.

17. **Haddon, Mark.** My Working Day. *The Guardian Review.* 07 07 2016, p. 5.

18. **Taylor-Batty, Mark.** *About Pinter: the playwright and the work.* London : Faber and Faber, 2005.

19. **Hargreaves, David J., Dorothy E. Miell, & Raymond A.R. MacDonald.** *Musical Imaginations: Multidisciplinary Perspectives on Creativity, Performance, and Perception.* Oxford & New York : Oxford University Press, 2012.

20. **Cocking, J.M.** *Imagination: A Study in the History of an Idea.* London & New York : Routledge, 1991.

21. **Hamilton, Andy.** The Aesthetics of Artistic Collaboration. Book auth. Martin Blain & Helen J. Minors. *Artistic Research in Performance through Collaboration.* Cham, Switzerland : Palgrave Macmillan, 2021, pp. 59-74.

22. **Becker, Howard S.** *Art Worlds.* Berkeley CA & London : University of California Press, 2008.

23. **Sawyer, Keith & Stacy DeZutter.** *Distributed creativity: how collective creations emerge from collaboration2, 2009,* Psychology of Aesthetics, Creativity, and the Arts, Vol. 3, pp. 81-92.

24. **Clarke, Eric F. & Mark Doffman.** *Distributed Creativity: Collaboration and Improvisation in Contemporary Music.* Oxford : Oxford University Press, 2017.

25. **Sloman, Steven & Philip Fernbach.** *The Knowledge Illusion: Why We Never Think Alone.* New York : Farrar, Strauss, and Giroux, 2011.

26. **Lindon, Adam & Eric F. Clarke.** Distributed cognition, ecological theory and groups improvisation. Book auth. Eric F. Clarke & Mark Doffman. *Distributed Creativity: Collaboration and Improvisation in Contemporary Music.* Oxford : Oxford University Press, 2017, pp. 52-69.

27. **Sawyer, R. Keith.** Emergence in Creativity and Development. Book auth. R. Keith Sawyer, Vera John-Steiner, Seana Moran, Robert J. Sternberg, David Henry Feldman, Jenne Nakamura, & Mihalyi Csikszentmihalyi. *Creativity and Development.* Oxford & New York : Oxford University Press, 2003, pp. 12-60.

28. **Till, Nicholas.** *Mozart and the Enlightenment: Truth, Virtue and Beauty in Mozart's Operas.* London : Faber and Faber Ltd., 1992.

29. **Cook, Nicholas.** *Music as Creative Practice.* Oxford : Oxford University Press, 2018.

30. **Konečni, Vladimir J.** Composers' Creative Process: the Role of Life-events, Emotion and Reason. Book auth. David J. Hargreaves, Dorothy E. Miell & Raymond A.R. MacDonald. *Musical Imaginations: Multidisciplinary perspectives on creativity, performance, and perception.* Oxford : Oxford University Press, 2012, pp. 141-155.

31. **Fontaine, Sheryl I. & Susan M. Hunter.** *Collaborative Writing in Composition Studies.* Boston MA and London : Thomson Wadsworth, 2006.

32. **Kounios, John & Mark Beeman.** *The Eureka Factor: Creative Insights and the Brain.* London : Windmill Books, 2015.

33. **Libert, Benjamin.** *Mind Time: The Temporal Factor in Consciousness.* Cambridge MA : Harvard University Press, 2004.

34. **Costandi, Moheb.** *Body I Am: The New Science of Self-Consciousness.* Cambridge MA : The MIT Press , 2022.

35. **Davies, Jim.** *Imagination: The Science of Your Mind's Greatest Power.* New York : Pegasus Books Ltd, 2019.

36. **Sartre, Jean-Paul.** *The Imaginary.* Trans. A. Elkäim-Sartre & J. & Webber. London & New York : Routledge, 2004.

37. **Koestler, Arthur.** *The Act of Creation.* London : Picador, 1975.

38. **Jobs, Steve.** Goodreads. 2000. https://www.goodreads.com/quotes/1031045-creativity-is-just-connecting-things-when-you-ask-creative-people. [Viewed: 1 12 2022.]

39. **Diamond, Marian C., David Krech & Mark R. Rosenzweig.** *The effects of an enriched environment on the histology of the rat cerebral cortex.* August 1964, Journal of Comparative Neurology, Vol. 123, pp. 111-20.

40. **Magsamen, Susan & Ivy Ross.** *Your Brain on Art: How the Arts Transform Us.* Edinburgh : Canongate, 2023.

41. **Wilson, Clare.** Lack of neuron 'pruning' behind many brain-related conditions. *New Scientist.* 29th April 2023, Vol. 258, 3436, p. 10.

42. **Barrett, Lisa Feldman.** *Seven and a half Lessons about the Brain.* London & Dublin : Picador, 2021.

43. **Webber, Jonathan.** Philosophical Introduction. Book auth. Jean-Paul Sartre. Trans. Arlette Elkäim-Sartre & Jonathan Webber. *The Imaginary.* London & New York : Routledge, 2004, pp. xiii-xxvi.

---

44. **Otten, Marte, Anil K Seth & Yair Pinto.** *Seeing Ɔ, remembering C: Illusions in short-term memory.* 4, April 2023, PLoS One, Vol. 18.

45. **Hills, Alison & Alexander Bird.** *Against Creativity.* 3, 2019, Philosophy and Phenomenological Research, Vol. 9, pp. 694-713.

46. **Carroll, Noël.** Art, Creativity, and Tradition. Book auth. Berys Gaut & Paisley Livingstone. *The Creation of Art: New Essays in Philosophical Aesthetics.* Cambridge & New York : Cambridge University Press, 2003, pp. 208-234.

47. **Merker, Björn H.** Layered Constraints on the Multiple Creativities of Music. Book auth. Irène Deliège & Geraint A. Wiggins. *Musical Creativity: Multidisciplinary Research in Theory and Practice.* Hove & New York : Psychology Press, 2006, pp. 25-41.

48. **Sawyer, R. Keith.** Introduction. Book auth. R. Keith Sawyer, Vera John-Steiner, Seana Moran, Robert J. Sternberg, David Henry Feldman, Jenne Nakamura, Mihalyi Csikszentmihalyi. *Creativity and Development.* Oxford & New York : Oxford University Press, 2003, pp. 1-11.

49. **Beard, Alex.** *Natural Born Learners.* London : Weidenfeld & Nicholson, 2017.

50. **Spencer, John P., Laia Fibla, Samuel H. Forbes, Jordan McCarthy, Kate Mee, Vincent Magnotta, Sean Deoni & Donnie Cameron.** *Language exposure and brain myelination in early development.* 15 May 2023, Journal of Neuroscience, p. 1034.

51. **Kuhl, Patricia K., Feng-Ming Tsao & Huei-Mei Liu.** *Foreign language experience in infancy: Effects of short-term exposure and social interaction on phonetic learning.* 15, 2003, Proceedings of the National Academy of Sciences of the United States, Vol. 100, pp. 9096-9101.

52. **Moran, Seana & Vera John-Steiner.** Creativity in the Making: Vygotsky's Contemporary Contribution to the Dialectic of Development and Creativity. Book auth. R. Keith Sawyer, Vera John-Steiner, Seana Moran, Robert J. Sternberg, David Henry Feldman, Jenne Nakamura, & Mihalyi Csikszentmihalyi. *Creativity and Development.* Oxford & New York : Oxford University Press, 2003, pp. 61-90.

53. **Freud, Sigmund.** Creative writers and day-dreaming. Ed. Peter Gay. *The Freud reader.* New York : Norton, 1989, pp. 436-443.

54. **Buzsáki, György.** *The Brain from Inside Out.* Oxford & New York : Oxford University Press, 2019.

55. **Damasio, Antonio.** *Descartes' Error: Emotion, Reason and the Human Brain.* London : Vintage Books, 2006.

56. **Mahn, Holbrook & Vera John-Steiner.** The Gift of Confidence: A Vygotskian View of Emotions. Book auth. Gordon Wells & Guy Claxton. *Learning for life in the 21st century: Sociocultural perspectives on the future of education.* Oxford : Blackwell, 2002, pp. 46-58.

57. **Noordhof, Paul.** *Imagining, Expressive Perception as Projective.* 2008, Mind and Language, pp. 329-358.

58. **Damasio, Antonio.** *The Strange Order of Things.* New York : Pantheon Books, 2018.

59. **Dickson, Andrew.** Shock treatments. *The Guardian Review.* 25 03 2017, p. 15.

60. **Bakhtin, Mikhail.** *The Dialogic Imagination.* Trans. Caryl Emerson & Michael Holquist. Austin : University of Texas Press, 1981.

61. **James, William.** *The principles of psychology, Vol. 1.* London : Macmillan, 1890.

---

62. **Hermans, Hubert J.M., & Harry J.G. Kempen.** *The Dialogical Self: Meaning as Movement.* San Diego CA : Academic Press, 1993.

63. **Hadamard, Jaques.** *The psychology of invention in the mathematical field.* New York : McGraw-Hill, 1945.

64. **Ghiselin, Brewster.** *The Creative Process: A Symposium.* Berkeley CA : University of California Press, 1952.

65. **Fernyhough, Charles.** *The Voices Within.* London : Profile Books, 2016.

66. **McCartney, Paul.** *The Lyrics: 1956 to the Present.* Ed. Paul Muldoon. London & New York : Penguin, 2021.

67. **Bailes, Freya, & Laura Bishop.** Musical Imagery in the Creative Process. Book auth. Dave Collins. *The Act of Musical Composition.* Farnham and Burlington VT : Ashgate, 2012, pp. 53-79.

68. **Predota, George.** How Inspiration Strikes. *Interlude.* 2019. http://www.interlude.hk/front/inspiration-strikes/. [Viewed: 07 05 2019.]

69. **Descartes, René.** *The Philosophical Works of Descartes.* Ed. Elizabeth S. Haldane & R.T. Ross. Cambridge : Cambridge University Press, 1970. Vol. Vol 1.

70. **Kross, Ethan.** *Chatter: The Voice in Our Head (and How to Harness It).* London and New York : Vermillion, 2022.

71. **Smith, Steven M., Thomas B. Ward & Ronald A. Finke.** Introduction: Cognitive Processes in Creative Contexts. Book auth. Steven M. Smith, Thomas B. Ward & Ronald A. Finke. *The Creative Cognition Approach.* Cambridge MA : MIT Press, 1995, pp. 1-8.

72. **Rossman, Joseph.** *The Psychology of the Inventor: A Study of the Patentee.* Washington DC : Inventor Publishing Co., 1931.

73. **Cameron, Julia.** *The Artist's Way: A Spiritual Path to Higher Creativity.* London : Souvenir Press, 2020.

74. **Parnes, Sidney J., Ruth B. Noller, & Angelo M. Biondi.** *Guide To Creative Action.* New York : Charles Scribner's Sons, 1977.

75. **Lucretius.** *On the Nature of Things.* Ed. Martin F. Smith. Trans. W. H. D. Rouse. Cambridge, MA : Loeb Classical Library, 1924.

76. **Mandler, George.** Origins and Consequences of Novelty. Book auth. Steven M. Smith, Thomas B. Ward & Ronald A. Finke. *The Creative Cognition Approach.* Cambridge MA : MIT Press, 1995, pp. 9-25

77. **Barthes, Roland.** Image Music Text, Trans. Stephen Heath. London : Fontana, 1977, pp. 142-148.

78. **Genders, Carolyn.** *Sources of Inspiration.* London & New York : Herbert Press , 2021.

79. **Chekhov, Anton.** Good Reads. 2022. https://www.goodreads.com/quotes/450250-if-you-want-to-work-on-your-art-work-on. [Viewed: 17 3 2022.]

80. **Damasio, Antonio.** Some Notes on Brain, Imagination and Creativity. Book auth. Valerie R. Shubik & Karl H. Pfenninger. *The Origin of Creativity.* Oxford & New York : Oxford University Press, 2001, pp. 59-68.

81. **Neruda, Pablo.** *Confieso que he vivido.* Barcelona : Seix Barral, 1974.

82. **Roe, Anne.** *Early Determinants of Vocational Choice.* 1957, Journal of Counseling Psychology, Vol. 4, pp. 212-217.

83. **Chiu, Chi-yue & Angela Ka-yee Leung.** *Do Multicultural Experiences Make People More Creative? If So, How?* The Inquisitive Mind, 4, 2007.

84. **Maddux, William W. & Adam D. Galinsky.** *Cultural borders and mental barriers: the relationship between living abroad and creativity.* May 2007, Psychology, Medicine; Journal of personality and social psychology, pp. 1047-61.

85. **Leung, Angela Kay-y, William W. Maddux, Adam D. Galinsky & Chiu-yue Chiu.** *Multicultural experience enhances creativity: The when and how.* 3, 2008, American Psychologist, Vol. 63, pp. 169–181.

86. **Reybrouck, Mark M.** Musical Creativity between Symbolic Modelling and Perceptual Constraints: The Role of Adaptive Behaviour and Epistemic Autonomy. Book auth. Irène Deliège & Geraint A. Wiggins. *Musical Creativity: Multidisciplinary Research in Theory and Practice.* Hove & New York : Psychology Press, 2006, pp. 42-59.

87. **Wallas, Graham.** *The Art of Thought.* London : C.A. Watts & Co., 1945.

88. **Leith, Sam.** Jeff VanderMeer. *Guardian Review.* 17 04 2021, pp. 17-19.

89. **Getzels, Jacob & Mihalyi Csikszentmihalyi.** *The Creative Vision: A Londitudinal Study of Problem Finding in Art.* New York : John Wiley, 1976.

90. **Forster, E.M.** *Howards End.* London : Penguin Classics, 2000.

91. **Liu, Lu, Nima Dehmamy, Jillian Chown, C. Lee Giles & Dashun Wang.** *Understanding the onset of hot streaks across artistic, cultural, and scientific careers.* September, 2021, Nature Communications, Vol. 12, Unpaginated web Journal.

92. **Smith, Steven M.** Fixation, Incubation, and Insight in Memory and Creative Thinking. Book auth. Steven M. Smith, Thomas B. Ward & Ronald A. Finke. *The Creative Cognition Approach.* Cambridge MA : 1995, pp. 135-56.

93. **Finke, Ronald.** *Imagery, Creativity and Emergent Structure.* 1996, Consciousness and Cognition, pp. 381-93.

94. **Soyinka, Wole.** This book is my present to Nigeria. *The Guardian Books,* 25.09.2022, pp. 56-57.

95. **Dijksterhuis, Ap & Teun Meurs.** *Where Creativity Resides: The Generative Power of Unconscious Thought.* 2006, Consciousness and Cognition, Vol. 15, pp. 135-146.

96. **Oppezzo, Marily & Daniel L. Schwartz.** *Give Your Ideas Some Legs: The Positive Effect of Walking on Creative Thinking.* 4, 2014, Journal of Experimental Psychology: Learning, Memory, and Cognition, Vol. 40, pp. 1142–1152.

97. **Wong, May.** Stanford study finds walking improves creativity - a press summary of the research article. 24 04 2014. https://news.stanford.edu/2014/04/24/walking-vs-sitting-042414/. [Viewed: 23 03 2022.]

98. **Wagner, Ullrich, Steffen Gais, Holde Haider, Rolf Verleger, & Jan Born.** *Sleep Inspires Insight.* 6972, 2004, Nature, Vol. 427, pp. 352–5.

99. **Stickgold, R., J.A. Hobson, R. Fosse & M. Fosse.** *Sleep, Learning, and Dreams: Off-line Memory Reprocessing.* 2001, Science, Vol. 294, pp. 1052–7.

100. **Lacaux, Célia, Thomas Andrillon, Céleste Bastoul, Yannis Idir, Alexandrine Fonteix-Galet, Isabelle Aarnulf & Delphine Oudiette.** *Sleep onset is a creative sweet spot.* 2021, Science Advances, Vol. 50:7.

101. **Ainsworth-Land, Vaune.** *Imagery and Creativity: an Integrating Perspective.* 1, 1982, The Journal of Creative Behaviour, Vol. 16, pp. 5-28.

102. **Sakkal, George J.E.** *Whose Truth, Whose Creativity? Why postmodern art theory is a culturally damaging mistake and how neuroscience can prove this.* London : The Black Spring Press group, 2021.

103. **Dewey, John.** *How we Think: a Restatement of the Relation of Reflective Thinking to the Educative Process.* Heath : Boston MA, 1933.

104. **Zedelius, Claire M., & Jonathan W. Schooler.** *Mind Wandering "Ahas" versus Mindful Reasoning: Alternative*

Routes to Creative Solutions. 2015, Frontiers in Psychology, Vol. 6, Unpaginated web journal.

105. **Henriksen, Danah, Carmen Richardson, & Kyle Shack.** *Mindfulness and creativity: Implications for thinking and learning.* September 2020, Thinking Skills and Creativity, Vol. 37, Unpaginated web journal.

106. **Mann, Sandi & Rebekah Cadman.** *Does Being Bored Make us more Creative?* 2014, 2, Creativity Research Journal, Vol. 26, pp. 165-73.

107. **Baird, Benjamin, Jonathan Smallwood, Michael D. Mrazek, Julia Kam, Michael S. Franklin, & Jonathan W. Schooler.** *Inspired by Distraction: Mind-wandering Facilitates Creative Incubation.* 2012, 10, Psychological Science, Vol. 23, pp. 1117-1122.

108. **Kaschub, Michele.** *Exercising the Musical Imagination.* 1997, 3, Music Educators Journal, Vol. 84, pp. 26-32.

109. **Webster, Peter R.** *Creativity as Creative Thinking.* 1990, 9, Music Educators Journal, Vol. 76, pp. 22-28.

110. **Copland, Aaron.** *Music and Imagination.* Cambridge : Harvard University Press., 1953.

111. **Vatansever, Deniz, David K. Menon & Emmanual A. Stamatakis.** *Default Mode Contributions to Automated Information Processing.* 2017, 48, Proceedings of the National Academy of Sciences USA, Vol. 114, pp. 12821-6.

112. **Jarosz, Andrew F., Gregory J.H. Colflesh, & Jennifer Wiley.** *Uncorking the muse: Alcohol intoxication facilitates creative problem solving.* 2012, 1, Consciousness and Cognition, Vol. 21, pp. 487-493.

113. **Haase, Jennifer, Paul Hanel, & Norbert, A. Gronau.** *Meta-Analysis, Creativity Enhancement Methods for Adults.* Psychology of Aesthetics, Creativity, and the Arts, 2022.

114. **Burke, Sean.** *The Death and Return of the Author.* Edinburgh : Edinburgh University Press, 2008.

115. **Harkaway, Nick.** I have a Firework going off in my Head and I have to Describe it. *The Guardian Review.* 11 11 2017, p. 11.

116. **Bowers, Kenneth S., Peter Farvolden, & Lambros Mermigis.** Intuitive Antecedents of Insight. Book auth. Steven M. Smith, Thomas B. Ward & Ronald A. Finke. *The Creative Cognition Approach.* Cambridge MA : 1995, pp. 27-52.

117. **Haught-Tromp, Catrinel.** *The Green Eggs and Ham hypothesis: How constraints facilitate creativity.* 2017, Psychology of Aesthetics, Creativity, and the Arts, Vol. 11, pp. 10–17.

118. **Bright, Jim & Robert G. L. Pryor.** Limitations and Creativity: A Chaos Theory Perspective December. 2015. https://www.researchgate.net/publication/. [Viewed: 25 02 2022.]

119. **Galinsky, Adam D. & Gordon B. Moskowitz.** *Counterfactuals as Behavioral Primes: Priming the Simulation Heuristic and Considerations of Alternatives.* 2000, Journal of Experimental Social Psychology, Vol. 36, pp. 384-409.

120. **Galinsky, Adam D., Gordon B. Moskowitz & Ian Skurnik.** *Counterfactuals as self-generated primes: The effect of prior counterfactual activation on person perception judgements.* Fall, 2000, Social Cognition, Vol. 18, pp. 252-280.

121. **Schoenberg, Arnold.** *Style and Idea: Selected Writings of Arnold Schoenberg.* Ed. Leonard Stein. Trans. Leo Black. Berkley CA : University of California Press, 1975.

122. **Saariaho, Kaija.** A Conversation with Kajia Saariaho; Interview with Clément Mao-Takas. *Music & Literature, Vol. 5.* 9 2014. http://www.musicandliterature.org/features/2014/9/22/a-conversation-with-kaija-saariaho. [Viewed: 19 6 2017.]

123. **Schooler, Jonathan W. & Joseph Melcher.** The Ineffability of Insight. Book auth. Steven M. Smith, Thomas

B. Ward & Ronald A. Finke. *The Creative Cognition Approach.* Cambridge MA : 1995, pp. 98-133.

124. **Gazzaniga, Michael S.** The Split Brain Revisited. *Scientific American.* July 1998, Vol. 279, 1, pp. 26-31.

125. **Gazzaniga, Michael S.** Sphere of Influence. *Scientific American Mind.* June/July 2008, Vol. 19 , 3, pp. 32-39.

126. **McGilchrist, Iain.** *The Master and his Emissary: The Divided Brain and the Making of the Western World.* New Haven & London : Yale University Press, 2009.

127. **Horace.** The Art of Poetry. Trans. Penelope Murray & T.S. Dorsch. *Classical Literary Criticism.* London : Penguin Books, 2000, pp. 98-112.

128. **Beardsley, Monroe C.** *On the Creation of Art.* 1965, Journal of Aesthetics and Art Criticism, Vol. 23, pp. 291-304.

129. **Adolfe, Bruce.** With Music in Mind. Book auth. Karl H. Pfenninger & Valerie R. Shubik. *The Origin of Creativity.* Oxford & New York : Oxford University Press, 2001, pp. 69-88.

130. **Kang, Yul H.R., Frederike H. Petzschner, Daniel M. Wolpert & Michael N. Shadlen.** *Piercing of Consciousness as a Threshold-Crossing Operation.* 2017, Current Biology, Vol. 27, pp. 1-11.

131. **McCutchan, Ann.** *The Muse that Sings: Composers Speak about the Creative Process.* Oxford : Oxford University Press, 1999.

132. **Tinio, Pablo L.** *From Artistic Creation to Aesthetic Reception: The Mirror Model of Art.* 3, 2013, Psychology of Aesthetics, Creativity, and the Arts, Vol. 7, pp. 265-275.

133. **Bever, Thomas & Robert J. Chiarello.** *Cerebral Dominance in Musicians and Non-musicians*1974, Science, Vol. 185, pp. 537-9.

134. **Cawelti, Scott, Allen Rapport & Bill Wood.** *Modelling artistic creativity: An empirical study.* 1992, 2, Journal of Creative Behaviour, Vol. 26, pp. 83-94.

135. **Deliège, Irène & Geraint A. Wiggins.** Prelude. Book auth. Irène Deliège & Geraint A. Wiggins. *Musical Creativity: Multidisciplinary Research in Theory and Practice.* Hove & New York : Psychology Press, 2006, pp. 1-6.

136. **Lotze, Martin, Gabriela Sheler & Nils Birbaumer.** From Music Perception to Creative Performance: Mapping Cerebral Differences between Professional and Amateur Musicians. Book auth. Irène Deliège & Geraint A. Wiggins. *Musical Creativity: Multidisciplinary Research in Theory and Practice.* Hove & New York : Psychology Press, 2006, pp. 275-289.

137. **Marsh, Diane T. & Judith Vollmer.** *The Polyphonic Creative Process: Experiences of Artists and Writers.* 1991, 2, Journal of Creative Behaviour, Vol. 25, pp. 106-115.

138. **Collins, Dave.** *A Synthesis Process Model of Creative Thinking in Musical Composition.* 2005, 2, Psychology of Music, Vol. 33, pp. 193-216.

139. **Katz, Shira L. & Howard Gardner.** Musical Materials or Metaphorical Models? A Psychological Investigation of what Inspires Composers. Book auth. David J. Hargreaves, Dorothy E. Miell & Raymond A.R. MacDonald. *Musical Imaginations: Multidisciplinary perspectives on creativity, performance, and perception.* Oxford : Oxford University Press, 2012, pp. 107-123.

140. **Glazner, Nancy.** Dialogic subversion: Bakhtin, the novel and Gertrude Stein. Book auth. Ken Hirschkop & David Shepherd. *Bakhtin and Cultural Theory.* Manchester : Manchester University Press, 2001, pp. 155-176.

141. **Shepherd, David.** Bakhtin and the reader. Book auth. Ken Hirschkop & David Shepherd. *Bakhtin and Cultural*

Theory. Manchester : Manchester University Press, 2001, pp. 136-154.

142. **Wolford, George, Michael Miller & Michael S. Gazzaniga.** *The Left Hemisphere's Role in Hypothesis Formation,* 2000, 6, Journal of Neuroscience, Vol. 20, pp. 1–4.

A number of alternatives to, or elaborations on, Wallas's four stages have been proposed. For instance, Tinio suggested three stages consisting of:

- Initialisation: '... the genesis of a concept and its initial expression as an artwork ...' (132 p. 267). Tinio argued that these are closely linked.

- Expansion and adaptation, which: '... involves the development and fine-tuning of aspects of an artwork that were established during the initialization stage.' (132 p. 268-9).

- Finalising, which: '... involves enhancements and modifications that signal the completion of the art-making process.' (132 p. 269).

The first of these, Initialisation, corresponds with the first three stages of Wallas's model, when a concept is developed and ideas emerge. Tinio was clearly covering more than one step in this stage, since he referred to the genesis of a concept, and then to its initial expression. Tinio's second and third stages represent a subdivision of the final stage in Wallas's model, verification.

Neurological evidence on the stage of illumination or inspiration was presented by Kounios and Beeman. They drew on many studies using brain imaging to show which parts of the brain light up when the moment of inspiration occurs. They described the process as having four stages, which correspond to the first three stages of the Wallas model, with the addition of a stage when progress is blocked. They omitted the stage of verification, since that was not the subject of their study. Their stages were: Immersion – in all aspects of the problem; Impasse – no idea how to proceed; Diversion – break from the problem; Illumination. (32 pp. 17-18)

Cawelti, Rapport, and Wood described stages of centring, expanding, creating, revitalising, distancing/reviewing/separating, evaluating, restarting (134 p. 89). This reads as a more complex re-expression of the Wallas stages of preparation, incubation, inspiration and verification. They also pointed out that people may not experience distinct stages, due to the complexity of the imaginative process.

The same qualification is made by Perkins (6 pp. 183-5), who wrote that 'Creative processes in fact cannot be understood as occurring in stages, and that such models misrepresent the multifaceted, highly complex, unpredictable activities required to create.' 134 p. 93). Certainly, models such as Wallas's simplify the process, and that is the purpose of models after all. As I pointed out in Chapter 2, 'stages' would more accurately be described as activities, and as activities which may be carried out repeatedly, in many different orders, and intermingled one with another.

Katz and Gardener questioned the rigidity of the stage model in music since 'Stage theory does not address what is happening in [musical] composers' minds from a cognitive psychological perspective nor does it provide in-depth information about the nature and sources of their inspiration' (139 p. 120), that is that stage theories don't take account of the content of the creative process. However, the models concern the form of the imaginative process and not its content. I don't see their criticism as valid.

Similarly, I don't see the argument that the process is too fluid to be described as a series of stages, made by Diane Marsh and Judith Vollmer (137), as invalidating the idea of stages. In their study, they asked a sample of twenty-five artists and writers to describe their creative processes, and then they comment on various conceptions of the process. The implication of their discussion is that artists perceive their processes as fluid rather than consisting of a neatly separable series of stages.

This does not negate the idea that there are different types of activity which take place within imaginative work. My argument in Chapter 2 is that, while you may not initially perceive distinct activities since they do tend to flow into one another, it will help you improve your imaginative skills if you are aware of Walls' model. You may then see that, while you may experience imagining as a continuous process, it does in fact have separate components.

If you then learn to slow down and analyse the process, this could open the door to taking on board that there are many methods which you could use to help with the different parts of the process and enable to find better ideas.

A separate criticism of Wallas's approach is that he based his model on accounts by scientists and mathematicians, and so the model may not apply to other fields. Irène Deliège and Geraint Wiggins made this point, arguing that scientists may discover an existing relationship, but do not claim to be inspired (135 p. 3). Again, I disagree, since the essential similarity between artist and scientist is that they may suddenly see a new relationship or possibility. As Koestler (37) and Read (4) argued, the imaginative processes they follow are essentially the same.

While there has been debate on the details of the stages or activities within imagining, it is widely accepted that imagining consists of several activities. For instance, Dave Collins looked at a series of models of imagination and compared them with studies of how composers worked. He concluded by suggesting a combination of a series of stages and moments of insight (138 pp. 207-8).

Taken together, these variations on, and critiques of Wallas proposal lead me to the conclusion that it is remarkably robust, especially if it is borne in mind that he was suggesting a model of the process of having a single idea rather than one of the whole of the imaginative process.

Printed in Great Britain
by Amazon

27934590R00053